MonologuesToGo
Presents

75 New Monologues Kids Will Love!

MonologuesToGo
Presents

75 New Monologues Kids Will Love!

Joyce Storey & Talia Pura

Foreword by Bob Luke

ISBN: 0-9994895-0-X
ISBN 13: 978-0-9994895-0-5

Library of Congress Control Number: 2017916805
Joyce Storey Productions, Inc., New York, NY

Book Cover by John Scott
Book Editor: Catherine McHugh
Graphic Designer: John Scott
Cover Photo: iStock.com

First edition

For information contact: info@monologuestogo.com

PRAISE FOR

75 New Monologues Kids Will Love!

I love this collection of monologues for kids, and know that the young actor in your family will love it even more. Ms. Storey and Ms. Pura have enviable resumes, and draw upon two lifetimes of knowledge and practical experience to deliver a well-designed and much-needed resource for young actors. This is a collection with scope, breadth, and clarity. It belongs on the desk of every young acting student, teacher, school librarian, and audition coach. Congratulations to young actors everywhere; your road just got a little bit easier.

Mike Kimmel, Actor/Writer/Acting Coach
Actor: *Treme, Zoo, Game of Silence, Distant Vision, Cold Case, In Plain Sight, Breakout Kings, The Tonight Show with Jay Leno, Buffy the Vampire Slayer, Convergence, and Deep in the Heart*
Author: *Scenes for Teens, Acting Scenes for Kids and Tweens*

* * *

I love this book and it really hits home for me on multiple levels. When I studied drama at college, we learned a lot of technique, method and history, but nothing to prepare us for auditions. In *75 New Monologues Kids Will Love!* Joyce Storey and Talia Pura hit the mark in providing valuable and practical insight for child actors and their parents on what's involved, what's required and how to hone one's skills to succeed. They couple all of this with some wonderfully written dramatic and comedic monologues that will show a full range of emotion and ability that will wow agents and casting directors. Well done, Joyce and Talia!

Bob Tulipan, Manager/Producer/Writer
Author: *Rockin' in the New World: Taking Your Band From the Basement to the Big Time,* published by Sterling and a *Billboard Magazine* Top Pick
Concert and Festival Producer: The Police, Cheap Trick, Patti Smith and Judas Priest
Executive Producer: *An Actor Prepares*, starring Jeremy Irons and Jack Huston

* * *

As a private acting coach in New York City, part of my job is to equip my clients with the right tools to go out and not only meet casting directors and agents, but also have the right material to best show WHO they are and how THEY can be cast. Not an easy task, especially when it comes to kids. I want to thank Joyce and Talia for giving me a treasure trove to chose from. This book makes my job easier. Great job. Thank you!

Robert C. Kirk, Actor/Acting Coach/Writer
Over 60 film and television credits including: *Money Monster, Inside Man, Chuck, Wonder Wheel, Bull, Elementary, and Law & Order SVU*

* * *

Having coached young auditioning actors for several years in New York City, I keep up with useful tools that are available to help direct these talented actors. *75 New Monologues Kids*

Will Love! by Joyce Storey and Talia Pura is a tool that cannot be missed. In today's ever-changing market, it is up-to-date and full of wonderful step-by-step direction and advice for both young actors and their parents. Being prepared and knowing what to expect makes the process so much more enjoyable. Broken down for you by age and gender, the layout of this book makes it easy to find the right monologue for your needs and covers all points to help you lay down a strong foundation for your work. And what a selection of monologues! I agree with the writers' comment in the notes section that even if you are younger or older than the suggested age range, if any monologue "speaks" to you, you can make it your own. MonologuesToGo (the website) has been around for some time and I trust the brand. Know that you are getting great advice and monologues from two talented women who care.

James Joseph Aquino, Actor/Acting Coach,
SAG-AFTRA, AEA
Seen on: *The Tonight Show with Jay Leno* and *Late Night with David Letterman*, and in films with Eli Wallach and Martin Landau
He has taught "The Business Side of Acting" in both New York and Chicago.

*   *   *

Longtime actors and drama teachers Joyce Storey and Talia Pura have put together an exceptional book filled with wonderful monologues for students. This kind of resource is hard to find and it is an exceptional tool for educators and students. I am always looking for good monologues to pass on to my students. Bravo to these two for assembling such a great acting tool for auditions.

Kayla Gordon, Director
Artistic Director of the Winnipeg Studio Theatre
Professor, University of Winnipeg

* * *

75 New Monologues Kids Will Love! presents a new
superlative abundance of diverse, compelling, and efficient
texts for young actors and students. It allows children
to truly follow Hamlet's advice to "speak the speech ...
trippingly on the tongue," not only due to the excellent,
wide-ranging pieces, but also because of the extraordinarily
helpful bonus tips from authors who understand both
acting and children. Kids — and their teachers and parents
— will love it as well as really learn from it, as it provides
a unique resource for the professional development of the
budding actor.

Patrick F. Gleason, Writer/Actor/Former Director, Digital
Film Academy, New York
Screenwriter: *To Die in Ireland* (Cavu Pictures)

* * *

This is such a great collection for kids and I'm so happy to
be a part of it. I teared up and laughed out loud on more
than one occasion while reading these monologues. Great
job, Joyce and Talia!

Catherine McHugh, New York City-based Editor/Writer
for various publications, including *Biography.com*, *Lighting
& Sound America*, *ARRAY magazine*, *TheStreet.com*, *Lighting
Dimensions*, and *Theatre Crafts International*

*   *   *

This is just what I needed when my daughter was young! She has always done well in theater and has now moved to New York to audition. Any young actor needs strong monologues to audition for agents and this book provides all sorts of great material. The monologues are really well written with many subjects to choose from. I love that there are tips for parents of child actors. They really help enormously. I wish I'd known a lot of this information when we first started out. I also love how the book is laid out so actors can easily look for monologues by age, type and gender. Thanks Joyce and Talia for writing this book. It's a gem.

Emmie House, Parent and former Co-President of the North Springs High School Drama Association in Atlanta, GA

DEDICATION

To young actors everywhere:
Follow your heart. It will never lead you astray.

TABLE OF CONTENTS

TABLE OF CONTENTS

FOREWORD

Working with child actors over the last 30 years (as both a performer and a teacher) has taught me a great many things.

One: There is no standard. They come in every shape, size, and color possible.

Two: They come in all ages — my clients have ranged from 3 to 87. I have always felt that the best adult actors still approach the art like kids. They use their imagination and joy to believe in the reality of the unreal, and to make every moment *fun*. Things children do naturally.

Three: None of them likes being underestimated (that is, treated like a child). This is especially true once they have decided to make the acting profession a job. They want to be taken seriously by their parents, relatives, and others around them. They are certainly not going to be treated like kids by the adults they work with on a professional stage or film set.

Taking steps to prepare themselves for an audition is important to them. They want the best training, advice they can understand, quality scripts, and audition material they can relate to — and that especially doesn't talk down to them.

Over the past several years, I have also seen many monologues written for kids that use overly simple situations and/or awkward kid slang, and that sound too much like an adult pretending to be below the age of 10. Many of them have come about as a result of talent conventions and showcases that require 1-to-2-minute monologues. Suddenly, to meet this need, everyone who ever claimed to be a teacher also decided that he or she could write a book, and, even more dangerously, a book of monologues for kids.

Recently, I received a message from an actor I worked with almost 20 years ago. Joyce was a very good actor: genuine, honest, and always real — both as a person and a performer. Lo and behold, she was working on a book — this one — and asked me to write the introduction. She thought my background as an on-set film and television coach who has found and developed actors from beginners to stars made me capable of evaluating the material and commenting on its real value.

The first thing I did was go to the people who I trust to be totally honest about what they need: the kids. I asked lots of different clients of various ages to read through these monologues, and tell me what they thought.

- **First**, they liked the material. The situations stretch from fantasy to actual problems and events that many had really gone through; all are relatable. Some of the more serious pieces touched them deeply, while many of the comedic ones made them laugh at themselves. They understood and identified with the work.

- **Second**, they felt the language was appropriate for their ages and sounded the way they and their friends talk. They didn't feel as if they were being forced to sound like a "gee whiz" TV kid from the 1950s.
- **Third**, these young actors felt they could use the material and make it their own. It was easy for them to express their own personalities instead of being constricted by the words.

Why are these things important? A lot has to do with what monologues are used for. What is their purpose?

We use monologues in acting classes to prompt students to develop their emotions, to learn to memorize lines when they aren't prompted by another's lines, to help build their confidence and stage presence, and to express them based on the story the words are telling in a realistic and believable way.

An audition monologue used to be the common way to show your skills at casting calls for theater plays. Currently, casting directors prefer to use "sides," which are the scripts from the actual production. However, use of the audition monologue is alive and well in meetings with agents and managers. And the younger the actors are, the more exciting it is to hear them do one they connect with and understand, and that enables them to show real emotions. This is exactly the reason this book was written the way it is.

Some actors can use the greatest words ever written and make them sound like they are ordering take-out from a fast food restaurant. Others can take a simple line, like a phrase from a greeting card, and make those who listen laugh and cry at the same time. Obviously, if you want to book a job, it is better to do the second one. How?

Many fine techniques or "methods" have been developed over the years to teach actors how to present an honest, well-acted performance. I have always taught a method based on common sense, and have often been heard to say, "Acting is simple; it just isn't easy. The hard part is keeping it simple!"
To avoid making the process sound difficult, I asked my young clients to put it in their own words:

- "Make it [the monologue] sound like a conversation by talking to someone you know."

This was expressed by a young actor of five, who understands to always make your monologue a natural conversation by making a specific choice as to who you are speaking and listening to — someone you know and would usually talk to about the story.

- "Don't rush through it, or recite it so you sound like a robot."

Good advice from an eight-year-old actor. A young teen added:

- "Take the time to listen to the other person, then try not to ramble your response, because they will stop listening to you."

The idea is that each monologue is your personal story. Understand it, and be able to express it so the meaning is clear. Just memorizing the words isn't enough. That can cause you to rush through it without thought or emotion. Make those listening to you understand and believe you!

What is it about the monologue that makes others feel the way you want them to? It's the emotions that you express. The purpose of a monologue from the agent or casting director's point of view is to show the actor's range of emotion. Be specific about the feelings you want to convey each time you perform, and demonstrate both positives (happiness, hope, love) and negatives (sadness, anger, confusion) so they can see what you are capable of.

Once again, it is important to remember you are in a conversation — you look and see your friend, you listen to them; that should make you *react* first, and then you *respond*. You will often find more emotions when reacting to your friend than from what the words are saying. What are you doing before your friend stops you and prompts you to tell them your story? Let them see what you are feeling even before the conversation starts — the opening emotions. And then, what are your reactions when you are done — the closing emotions?

- "If you make a mistake with the words, don't stop! Just keep going because no one else knows you messed up. Don't ever say, " I'm sorry." That just tells them you made a mistake!"

This is a quote all of my clients will tell you in one form or another. Who made the mistake? Was it the actor, or the character? When you believe in the story you are telling, you will not have a need to apologize.

In summary, I believe *75 New Monologues Kids Will Love!* by Joyce and Talia is written the way you speak and think. You should be able to find many that you like, several you can relate to, and some you may have already said to someone in your own words. These monologues are meant to be a starting point for your preparation, not the end. Your audience wants to see you: your personality, energy, naturalness, and your range of emotions. Take these words and situations, and build upon them to make them your own. Let them become your story through your interpretation and your emotions. If you believe in them, then so will we.

— Bob Luke
Director, The Bob Luke Acting Studio
New York City

Bob Luke is the Director of the Bob Luke Acting Studio, located in the heart of Manhattan's theater district. An accomplished actor in his own right, he has performed more than 80 stage and film roles and trained thousands of actors ranging in age from 3 to 87. Casting directors, agents, and managers across the country recommend him for commercial acting instruction, sitcom technique, audition preparation, and actor development. He counts being an on-set coach for the Disney live-action musical fairytale feature *Enchanted*, starring Amy Adams, Patrick Dempsey, and Susan Sarandon, among his numerous credits. Some of his award-winning clients include Josh Hutcherson (*The Hunger Games*), Sarah Michelle Gellar (*Buffy the Vampire Slayer*), Michelle Trachtenberg (*Harriet the Spy*), and Noah Fleiss (*Joe the King*).

ACKNOWLEDGMENTS

They say it takes a village — and it does. We are so very grateful to our friends and family who have been incredibly supportive during the writing and production of this book. A special thanks to our husbands, Howell Binkley and William Pura, for their support, patience, and guidance. Also, to Veda Storey for her many reviews of the material, wise edits, and undying enthusiasm for this project.

Many thanks to our wonderful editor Catherine McHugh, who has seen this book from seed to fruition with a keen eye and strong sense of structure, message, and content. Thanks to our wonderful graphic designer, John Scott. We are fortunate to have someone of your artistic talent and ability.

Thank you to those who have built the MonologuesToGo.com brand into a thriving community: David Hall, Molly Cameron, Umar Khokhar, Artisha Mann, Bonita Elery, Kristy Lyons, Taylor Vandick, Jessie McLaren, Farhan Gillani and RemoteLocalOffice.com, the wonderful team at Daily News Digital and, of course, our MtG writers. Special thanks to Mark Levine for seeing our potential in the early days and nurturing our growth. To Bobby Holder and the TAPNYC community, thanks for a phenomenal partnership.

To our dear friend Mike Kimmel who has been a guiding light throughout this project: Thank you for generously giving of your knowledge, time, and endless support. To Bob Tulipan, Robert Kirk, James Aquino, Patrick Gleason, Kayla Gordon, and Emmie House, thank you for taking the time and care to review this book and for lending your kind words.

Finally, a giant thanks to Bob Luke: You took so much time and care in reviewing this book and giving us detailed notes. Thank you for your thoughtful insights in writing the eloquent foreword and for generously workshopping our monologues with your amazingly talented students. Your contribution has been invaluable and your care and love for this project can never be repaid. We are truly grateful for every painstaking hour you have labored over this endeavor. You have elevated it to a level we could never have imagined. Thank you — thank you, thank you, thank you.

ABOUT THIS BOOK

This book is for you. It has been a labor of love for both of us. We love kids and we love theater! Both of us are professional actors, writers, and drama educators. We know what it's like to be on both sides of the audition table and we know what it takes to book an acting job. We know the euphoria of booking a role and the disappointment of not booking one. We've never given up and it has paid off for us. We have had so many exciting opportunities in our creative careers and we want you to have the same. Before you book anything, you need to hone your craft. Monologues are a wonderful tool for learning. They are also necessary tools for auditions. This book is our gift to you, the child actor. It will help you get off on the right foot. We have written about topics that interest and excite young people. Choose the monologues that "speak to you" — the ones you relate to, where you really feel you can bring your own style to the material. Have fun with the monologues and nurture your joy of acting!

Much love,
Joyce & Talia

HOW TO USE THIS BOOK

We have laid out this book to be as actor-friendly as possible.

Use the **table of contents** for quick reference. Find the title, type, length, age range and page number of each monologue quickly and easily.

Each monologue has its own individual page for easy learning. You can focus on one monologue at a time. Each one is isolated on its own page, so you can quickly glean information and memorize it.

Each monologue is **given an age range and gender** to help guide you. Please note that this is just that: a guide. If you connect with a monologue that is labeled outside of your age range, or designates male instead of female (or vice versa), you may alter it to suit your needs. You can still perform it. Put your own spin on it and make it your own. It will probably be perfect for you! If there is a reference to age within the monologue itself, you are welcome to change that number to suit your needs. Remember, these monologues are for YOU.

Monologues are **labeled either dramatic, comedic, or comedic/dramatic.** If you are looking for a specific type of monologue, simply scan the table of contents. They are all labeled there for quick reference.

A note about the **comedic/dramatic** monologues: Some monologues may be dramatic but still have humor. This is the case with many well-crafted monologues. If we felt there was a balance of both in a monologue, we labeled it comedic/dramatic. This gives the young actor even more opportunity to show the range of emotions he or she can bring to a piece.

Some monologues may have **incorrect grammar, spelling, or slang terms**. This is done on purpose, as it is meant to convey the way the character speaks and helps add a layer to the character you are creating.

There are very few **stage directions** in these monologues. This is intentional. They are designed for universal use, to allow for maximum flexibility of time and place. You, the actor, can choose the best location and time that works for you in that role. Be specific in your choices. They will enrich your work.

Though there are no specified **accents** in the stage directions for these characters, you are welcome to use various accents if they bring an added dimension to piece. A cautionary note, though: If you choose to use an accent, make sure you work with a dialect coach to polish it. If your accent sounds phony, DON'T use it. It will weaken your performance.

TIPS FOR PARENTS OF YOUNG ACTORS

CHILD ACTORS — WHERE TO BEGIN

Parents often have children who want to get into "the business" but have no idea how to go about it. The first thing we recommend is a good acting class. Raw talent is important, but having a teacher mold that talent and teach your child "the craft" of acting is essential. There are a lot of great acting studios. Find out who has the best reputation in your area. It will not only be a great learning experience from an acting standpoint, but your child will learn poise and public speaking skills that will help in other walks of life as well. It is also a wonderful community to be part of — and that's often where you hear about upcoming auditions.

"Winging it" will not serve your child well in an audition situation. Casting directors and agents expect children to be as prepared and professional for their auditions as adult actors. They may ask the child actor to improvise during an audition, but they also expect them to come into the room prepared with either "sides," which are the lines that have been given to the child prior to the audition, or a monologue. The sides should be well prepared, and if your child does not read well, he or she can memorize them. Memorizing is not, however, a necessity unless specified ahead of time.

The child actor should at all times have **at least two kids' monologues** prepared for auditions, one comedic and one dramatic. Even if the audition notice does not call for a monologue, casting directors or agents may ask for one once the actor is in the room.

The acting business requires a great deal of dedication on behalf of parents as well as children. If your child chooses to be an actor, you need to prepare him or her for the fact that even though it's a lot fun, it is also a discipline.

CHILD ACTORS' HEADSHOTS

A child actor, just like an adult, needs to have his tools in his pocket, so to speak. He or she needs an 8x10 color headshot (no one uses black and white anymore) that truly looks like him or her. That may sound a bit odd, but it is amazing how many headshots do not represent the true likeness of the child. Perhaps the child has grown or maybe her hair has been cut or restyled since the shot was taken. Because children change so quickly, we do not recommend spending exorbitant amounts of money on a headshot. It can cost more than $1,000 for some of the best headshot photographers. The pictures are gorgeous but you don't want to spend that kind of money when it will be outdated in a short amount of time.

Casting directors and agents know how quickly kids change and they do not expect you to spend that kind of money either. They do, however, expect a good quality shot that shows the personality of your child. A snapshot is not a headshot. The picture needs to look like a professional took it. If you know a good amateur who can make it look professional, that is fine. The important thing is to capture the essence of who the child is. For example, if he or she is mischievous, then try to catch that on film. Also, lighting is critical. Make sure there is a catch light in their eyes. (The light can come from the sun if it's an outdoor shoot.) The eyes are the most critical part of the shot. If they tell a story or create a mood, then it's probably a good shot. The child needs to look relaxed, open and natural. The picture should not look too "posed."

A good headshot is critical. It's the actor's calling card and often is what gets him or her the audition. They can't audition with one of the best-performed kids' monologues ever if they don't even get in the door! Make sure the headshot is first-class!

CHILD ACTORS' RESUMES

Many people are overwhelmed when it comes to creating a resume. Don't be. It's really not that scary. You can find samples online with a quick Internet search. First rule of thumb: Don't clog it up with too many words. Unlike other types of resumes, full sentences are not necessary for an acting resume. Put the pertinent information in columns and use 10- or 12-point type in a simple font. Your child's name (in big, bold letters), contact information and union status go at the top center. For safety reasons, we don't recommend including home numbers or addresses. A cell-phone number or manager/agent contact will suffice. Below that, usually on the left-hand side, list hair color, eye color, and height. Make sure you update your child's height as he or she grows.

Next, include show credits from the time the child started acting. Don't worry if there aren't a lot. If your child is only 7, she has not had time to gather many credits, but the ones she has are important. Be honest. Casting directors and agents have a way of knowing what is true and what is not. Credits should be listed by category as follows: THEATER, FILM, TELEVISION, TRAINING, SPECIAL SKILLS, and COMMERCIALS. Under this last category, simply put "Conflicts available upon request." Don't list individual commercials unless the actor has no other credits. If he doesn't have credits in a certain category, such as film, simply skip it. Also, you may put film or television higher than theater if those are the stronger credits. Theater credits usually go first in New York, whereas film and television credits are first in Los Angeles.

Credits are listed in three columns below each category. The first column is the project name, the second is the role or type of role, and the third is the production company. You can include the director's name if he is noteworthy. Here's an example:

THEATER

The Wizard of Oz	Dorothy	Roosevelt Elementary School

Training and special skills are valuable additions to your child's resume. If he is a good skateboarder, make sure to put that on the list. Maybe she can juggle or play the piano. Sometimes these skills are key to booking a role.

Attach the resume to the back of your child's picture. Use four staples, one neatly placed in each corner. You may also use a glue stick but sometimes glue dries out over time. It is best to have the actor's name on the front of the headshot in the bottom corner in case it gets separated from the resume.

Trim resumes to fit the 8x10 headshot. You can place an optional small photo in the upper corner so agents can see the actor's face while they read his credits. The most important thing is that the resume and headshot look professional so when the child actor walks in the door, the agent or casting director knows he is prepared and ready to book the job.

SELF-TAPING AUDITIONS

There are lots of instances where actors may go to a specified location for an audition — often the casting director's studio. However, with today's technology, it's become popular for casting directors to request that you tape your child's audition and email it to the casting studio. There are video taping studios where you can pay for your audition to be put on tape but you can easily do it yourself on your smartphone. You don't need to invest in expensive equipment. However, you do have to make sure that the audition is of the highest quality possible.

Choose a quiet, well-lit place in your home or office. The sound must be as clean and audible as possible. Natural light is great. You may also use practical fixtures such as a household lamp or overhead light. Just make sure that the light source does not cast shadows on your child actor's face. The face must be well lit and look natural. This is not the time for dramatic theatrical lighting. Your child should wear a solid color that brings out her natural color. If the shirt has a pattern, make sure it is not so busy that it distracts from the acting. Hold the camera steady in one position. This is about the acting, not the camera work. You may use a stool, table or tripod to steady the camera if desired. The angle should be straight on from the chest up. If you need to show hands, make the angle slightly wider but not more than waist high. You want the facial expression to be clearly visible.

Have your child "slate" his name, which is a fancy term for stating his name. It's important to do this in a friendly, open manner. It should be natural and easy.

The piece should be well rehearsed before she performs the material. Sometimes memorization is required.

Check with the agent or casting office to find out, as it can be a deal breaker if done incorrectly. The lines should never "sound memorized" like they're being recited. The audition is about the acting, not about how well a child can memorize. Casting Directors like to see an actor have the material memorized because they look confident and like they're having fun!

If it does not need to be completely memorized, the child needs to know the material well. The better he knows the material, the more comfortable he will be. It is not good to have his eyes drop down to the page and lose connection with the audience. Be sure the sides being read are held as close to eye level as possible, but out of the camera's view. Auditions need to sound as natural as if the child were telling you a story of her own.

You can do several takes. Usually, actors warm up and loosen up after one or two takes, so doing it several times is fine. Use the best version you have to send to the casting director. It's okay to coach your child between takes. You want to send the best product you can to the casting director. Remember, even if your child doesn't book this one, it's a chance to perform on camera and she increases her skill level by practicing. Also, the casting director may be impressed with your child's work, but he or she just may not be what the director is looking for. However, your child is now on the radar of the casting director for upcoming projects. One good audition can lead to another. And, sometimes, the child books the role and that is very exciting!

Have fun while taping auditions. Use it as a chance to perform and enjoy it!

CHILDREN'S MONOLOGUES

And now for the BIG question: "How do I help my child choose the perfect monologue?" That's easy — and not so easy. The right monologue has to fit like it was written for the child actor who is performing it. Whether performing for a teacher, classmates, casting director, agent, church congregation, family gathering, or anyone else, the actor needs to give an honest, entertaining portrayal of the character she has chosen. Look for material that your child can relate to. Maybe he finds it funny or, perhaps, she has had a similar experience to the character. You want something that the child actor is excited about working on, something that he or she will practice and be able to memorize. **Kids MUST always memorize their monologues.** They will NEVER be allowed to read from the paper.

A well-crafted kid's monologue will give the actor a chance to show various sides of his or her personality. If you are using the monologue for auditioning and professional purposes, it should be one to two minutes long, which is the industry standard. Sometimes the length is specified, depending on the audition. Ideally, your child will have two or three monologues of a contrasting nature prepared and ready to go at any moment. Monologues are a large part of the arsenal of "tools" every actor, no matter what age, should have prepared at all times. A carpenter would never show up at a job site without his tools, and neither should an actor.

You want to find a monologue that best brings out the child actor's personality. He needs to stand out among many, many other actors auditioning for the same role. Casting directors and agents are looking for the person with that "special something" that will win the heart of audiences. It is important that kids perform the monologues as if they truly are the characters they are portraying. It is not good enough to simply know the lines and recite them. She must become the character in every way possible. They should always have a coach help them to practice and shape their monologues. They need to be able to drop into the character within seconds of being asked to perform it. This is a skill they can learn and they must be able to repeat it consistently. This is their time to shine, so you want to help them choose a monologue that helps them do exactly that.

DRAMATIC MONOLOGUES

A strong dramatic monologue is critical to the success of a young actor's audition. Help your child choose a piece that really packs a punch and makes a memorable impression. A dramatic monologue should draw out a young actor's emotional range. The character should show different levels of emotion. An actor should take his audience on a two-minute journey that has such an impact on them, they remember it and think about it long after the actor has left the room. Well-written dramatic monologues give child actors the opportunity to delve deeply into the well of their talents and show their unique abilities to become the characters they are portraying. A character should go through a metamorphosis or discovery. It's not enough to simply play the surface emotion of the character. If a character is angry, for example, you need to find out why. Finding the nuances and depths of the emotion of a character is an actor's job. For example, there are many ways of playing anger besides yelling. Sometimes anger can come out very softly. Explore all the ways that work for you, and try to use more than one. Playing general anger serves neither the actor nor the material, and it certainly will not satisfy an audience. People are complex beings and an actor's performance should reflect this complexity. The higher the stakes, the better the performance. That's not to imply a performance should "appear" difficult. Raising the stakes simply means making the outcome more important to the character. Feelings and words should float from the page organically, as though the character is having the thought for the first time.

Our well-crafted dramatic monologues provide young actors with a blueprint for embarking on their character's exciting dramatic journey. The words will guide them as they peel away the layers of their character's rich inner life, allowing young actors to enjoy flexing their acting muscles! The more passionate young actors are about delving into the honesty of the character, the more likely they will be to touch their audiences and book the jobs!

COMEDIC MONOLOGUES

Your child's comedic monologue is a chance for him to show his lighter side as an actor. This does not mean he should take it less seriously than his dramatic work. Comedy is serious business! A comedic monologue needs to have just as much emotional depth as a dramatic one. Actors need to go on a journey with their characters and find the layers in the writing. It takes just as much work to be funny and entertaining as it does to be full of angst and dramatic tension. When looking for a comedic monologue, try to find something that calls to the young actor's personal sensibility.

We all have our own version of what tickles our funny bones. Have them pick something they connect to. They will save themselves and their acting coach a lot of time and soul-searching if they naturally relate to their material. They will also find they have more longevity with their comedic monologues if they genuinely find them amusing and enjoy playing the characters. There is a whole range of material in the world of comedic monologues. Some comedy is actually very dark. If your child actor has a flare for the dramatic and wants to add another layer to her work, she might look for something a little more on the dark comedic side.

Pick the brand of comedy that suits their type. A cute, girl-next-door type might want to choose a more light and airy style. Conversely, a more brooding type of guy would be better served by sticking to something that he is more likely to be cast in. Actors' material must fit them like tailor-made outfits. Young actors need to become the characters in comedy, just as in drama. And, as an added bonus, they get to make their audiences laugh!

75 New Monologues Kids Will Love!

A BAD WEEK

Female Dramatic
Age Range: 11 – 16
2 minutes   By Talia Pura

It's been a week since Zach dumped me. I have to stop thinking about him. He could do this thing with his eyes, this little squinty thing that made me fall head over heels in love with him — argh. STOP. (*big breath*) I'm over him. I am over him! In fact, I'm surprised at myself for ever thinking I loved him. A boyfriend, as far as I'm concerned, should be three things: Number 1: nice. If he weren't, he would be a complete waste of time. Number 2: He should be cute. If not, I couldn't fantasize about his cute face because he wouldn't be cute. And number 3: He has to be popular. Because if he were not popular, to go out with him would make everyone else dislike me. Zach was only one of those three things: popular. He wasn't nice, that's for sure. He'd go out with me, then dump me to see if he could go out with someone else and when they said no, he'd go out with me again. He was kind of using me for a back-up plan. And stupid me, I agreed to go out with him again because my obsession didn't allow me to see what a loser he was. And he wasn't even cute. True, he had those eyes, but his teeth were a mess and his head was kind of misshapen. I think I could do better. I can find someone who appreciates me and falls head over heels in love with me. Right now, I am promising myself that I will NOT go out with Zach again, even if he asks me to. He might — he's very unpredictable. Why is it so hard to stay away from someone, even when he is only a one out of three?

A DOG NAMED ROGER

Male/Female Dramatic
Age Range: 7 – 14
2 minutes   By Talia Pura

Last night I heard my mom and dad talking about Roger. He's been my very best friend since I was born. He is always happy to see me. He licks my face as soon as I get home from school. I used to take him outside every day, but he doesn't want to go for walks anymore. When I get his leash and say, "Come on, boy, let's go for a walk," he still gets excited. He wags his tail and looks at me, but then, he doesn't even stand up. It's because he's very old. I don't really understand how he got so old, when he's just the same age as me, but you have to count dog years differently than human years. In dog years, Roger is really, really old. He's so old that my mom and dad were talking about how long he was going to live. They didn't think I could hear them, but they were actually talking about bringing him to the vet and having him "put to sleep." That's what they called it, but I know what that means. I can't imagine Roger not being there when I come home from school. I heard my dad say that Roger is really suffering, and it isn't fair to let an animal suffer. Then my mom started to cry. She said she wasn't ready to say goodbye. That made me want to cry, too, but I know that I have to be brave and think of Roger. He's always been such a good dog. I don't want him to suffer to stay with us any longer. But then, how do you say goodbye to your very best friend?

A VAMPIRE PROTECTION CLUB

Male / Female Comedic
Age Range: 7 – 15
2 minutes   By Talia Pura

I'm thinking about starting a new club. There are lots
of clubs after school that I could join, but who cares
about playing chess or making a better science fair
project when there are so many vampires running
around looking for your blood? What my school really
needs is a vampire protection training club. We'd
meet every week — I think Wednesdays would be
best. That way we'd have time to get ready for the
weekend, which is prime vampire hunting time. I don't
know why vampires mostly come out on weekends,
but that's just the way it is. Our club could share tips
on keeping vampires at bay. Stringing garlic cloves
could be our first craft project. Then we'd learn how
to sharpen our wooden stakes. It's important that they
are very pointy at one end, because a vampire's heart
is pretty tough, and it's got to go right through it, or
you'll end up with fang marks on your neck, and never
remember how they got there. I, for one, don't want to
be forced to wear a turtleneck sweater to school every
day to hide that nasty bit of business so I've got to be
ready. Another important tip is to always go out in
pairs. Safety in numbers. Just make sure your walking
buddy is also a member of the club. Otherwise, you'll
just end up having to save both of you during an attack
because your friend won't know what to do, and
probably isn't even carrying silver, or a wooden stake,

or even garlic. I think maybe just the idea of a vampire protection training club would act as a safety measure. Any vampire who hears about our club is likely to choose a different neighborhood. He'd know he was beaten before he even started. Prevention is always the best cure.

A VAMPIRE SAFETY GUIDE

Male/Female Comedic
Age Range: 7 – 14
2 minutes   By Talia Pura

You already know that the best way to kill a vampire
is to drive a wooden stake into its heart. You'd have
to get pretty close to the vampire, though. Probably,
you'd get bitten yourself in the process. It might be
worth it, though, if say, the vampire was going after
somebody really cute that I wanted to impress. That
would be very noble, and becoming a vampire myself
would actually be pretty cool. But usually, you want to
save yourself from a vampire. My mom won't let me
carry a wooden stake with me at all times, so I have a
small tree branch in my backpack. That should do it
and my mom just thinks I'm into nature. And garlic —
always carry garlic, or eat a lot of it if you can stand
the taste. I also put a silver crucifix on my Christmas
list this year. My mom finds this pretty weird because
we aren't religious. I sure hope she doesn't buy some
cheap silver-plating, 'cause that's really not going to
do it. Ideally, I would tie the vampire up to a tree with
my silver chain and crucifix. That way it would be
exposed to sunlight the next morning, which would
totally fry it. Some people say vampires can get used to
sunlight and it just makes them sparkle, but that's just
not true. Sunlight will always burn them, which is why
my number one tip for avoiding death by vampires is
to just not go out at night. But hey, it gets dark pretty

early in the winter, so, if you follow my tips, you'll be safe... unless you really want to become a vampire yourself, in which case, you can just hang out at night and wait for one to bite you.

A VAMPIRE WARNING

Male/Female Comedic
Age Range: 7 – 15
2 minutes   By Talia Pura

There are 451 vampires in the world. I know this
because I read a lot of comic books. But don't worry,
you can protect yourself. Garlic keeps them away,
although I've heard some develop a taste for it. I know
I have. When I was a little kid, I hated garlic, but now
I love it. I tell my mom to add garlic to everything.
She refuses to put it into my breakfast cereal though,
which definitely puts me at greater risk walking to
school. Mom reminded me that vampires only come
out at night. Technically, that's true, but I don't like
to take chances. What if there was a vampire who
didn't make it home before daybreak and is hiding
out under some bushes I have to pass on my way to
school? You think that couldn't happen? I bet it has.
With that many vampires loose in the world, they could
be anywhere. I'm working hard on my S.A. — that
stands for situational awareness. I doubt very much
that a vampire could sneak up on me. One glimpse of
those white fangs and out comes my silver crucifix. It
won't kill it, but it will weaken it enough to fall down
and wait for the fatal thrust of my wooden stake. Yes, I
carry one at all times. That's just plain vampire basics.
It's the only sure way to kill one — except for sunlight,
but how are you going to convince a vampire to wait
around until the sun comes out when it wants your
blood now? So, always carry a stake, unless you're

against violence, and not sure you could actually follow through. If that's the case, just eat garlic, a lot of it, every day and no vampire will come within ten feet of you. Unfortunately, neither will anyone else, but that's a small price to pay for your safety.

A WEREWOLF INSIDE

Male/Female Comedic
Age Range: 7 – 14
2 minutes   By Talia Pura

I think maybe I'm a werewolf. It's true that I've never actually changed during a full moon, but that's not surprising. The signs don't start showing up until late in puberty. So, I'm probably just in the process of becoming a werewolf. There are only three ways that this can happen. The first one is the best. If you are born to parents that are werewolves, you are guaranteed to become one yourself. It's possible both of my parents are werewolves. I've never seen my mother turn — but she could have werewolf genes that she can pass on to me without being one herself. As for my dad, well, he always works the night shift. So far, I haven't heard any news reports about a werewolf going on a rampage while he's at work, but that doesn't mean he hasn't snuck off into a forest during a full moon. He's the night watchman at a factory. Who would know? Sometimes he seems kind of angry before he leaves for work, and then he is all calm and everything the next day. I haven't been bitten by a werewolf, and as far as I know, I haven't been cursed, so the only way I'm a werewolf is if I was born one. Now, I just have to wait to finish puberty to find out. If I am, I've already decided to use my powers to help people. You know, protect them from vampires and monsters or wild animals. There is no need to go crazy on people I love. Sometimes, during a full moon, I stare at my hands, waiting to see the veins pop and the hair start to grow. Nothing has happened yet, but I've got time. I've been practicing my howls at the moon, just in case. AWHOOOOOOOO!

ART FIELD TRIP

Male/Female Comedic
Age Range: 11 – 16
1.5 minutes   By Joyce Storey

I don't get art. We went on a field trip to this museum
and the teacher showed us a picture of some guy with
a face made of a shovel. I dunno, I guess someone
thought it was cool cuz the curator guy said it's worth
a bunch of thousands of dollars, but I have no idea
why. Imagine if he'd used a pitchfork or maybe a rake!
What would that be worth? Hey, maybe the guy should
make a whole series of 'em. He could make a killing!
Whoa! *I* should do it! I don't know if I can paint, but
how hard can it be? This guy wasn't so hot at it — the
handle on the shovel wasn't even straight. He had some
poetry or something scribbled all over his. Maybe I'll
get my friend, Tyrone to think up what to put. He's an
awesome rapper. He's got flow and all that. He could
scribble somethin' slick on it and he's got a cool tag he
could put on the bottom. And we could sell 'em out of
his big brother's car as long as they fit in the trunk. Oh,
and we could make a website! I can't wait to tell my
parents I'm dropping outta school to be an artist all cuz
they sent me on this field trip! They'll flip! Dad works
for IBM and Mom's an accountant. First, I'll announce
I'm not going to college, and then I'll spring my big
plan on them! It'll be priceless! I wish I had a hidden
camera so I could really get 'em goin' and then see their
reaction when I tell them they've been punked! Bet I
won't be goin' on any more field trips.

BABY PICTURE

Male/Female Dramatic
Age Range: 6 – 12
1 minute   By Talia Pura

My brother put my baby picture up on his bulletin board. He's four years older than me, and sometimes he's pretty mean. He doesn't let me play with him when his friends come over, and I can't keep up with him on my bike. But every time I go into his room, and see my baby picture up there on his wall, I know that he really does like me a lot. Then one day, my mom was helping him pack up his room because we were moving to a different house. She told him how nice it was that he hung up my picture. "What?" he asked, "That isn't me?" "No," she said, "I remember that outfit. I didn't buy it for you." When we moved to the new house, he never put my picture back up on the wall. I guess it sort of hurt my feelings, but maybe it shouldn't. I've never put up a picture of him, either.

BEACON BACON

Male/Female Comedic
Age Range: 6 – 11
1 minute   By Joyce Storey

Beacon and Dakota are cousins and Emma and I are cousins but I'm not cousins with Beacon and Dakota; just Emma. Beacon's name is pronounced Bee-can, not bacon like the breakfast meat. But sometimes kids call him bacon to be funny or something. He doesn't mind. He likes bacon. Me, too. I loooooove bacon! I could eat bacon every meal if Mom would let me. But she says it's got too much fat so I can only have three pieces at breakfast. I gobble down the first two and then I eat the last one as slow as I can to make it last. I like it cuz it's salty and yummy. Our dog, Dumbo, likes it, too. He's always begging when I eat it. I don't blame him. Sometimes I give him some but then I don't get as much and it's just sooooo good! Anyway, this is Beacon, not bacon and he's my friend, not my cousin.

BEDTIME

Male/Female Comedic
Age Range: 6 – 12
1 minute   By Talia Pura

You know how sometimes you just don't want to do as you're told? Why should you? Why should anyone get to tell someone else what to do just because they are older? Sometimes I just want to do what I want to do. I don't want to listen to adults. Do your homework. Take a bath. Go to bed. Turn off that light right now and go to sleep! Sometimes I don't want to go to sleep. Why should I go to bed if I'm not tired? (*big yawn*) Adults always think they know when you're tired. They don't. (*yawn*) I'm not even a little bit tired, and I'd rather watch TV, or play a video game, or read, or even do my homework than go to bed. I think I should be able to go to bed when I'm good and ready to go to bed (*yawning*) and not when my mom tells me to.

BFFs

Female Comedic
Age Range: 7 – 12
2 minutes   By Joyce Storey

Stacy texted Jody that you were BFFs with Karen now. Is that true? I thought you were my BFF. Remember we went behind the school and texted each other and did that thing with our pinkies and spit on our phones and everything? Didn't that mean anything to you? Cuz it was totally everything to me. My phone got all fogged up and stuff and my mom said it was from the moisture of the spit but I said it was worth it not to be able to read my texts anymore cuz I had my BFF Lauren now, but my mom swapped out my phone cuz she said for safety she wants me to be able to read my texts from her. Is that why you're not my BFF anymore? Cuz I swapped out the phone that I spit on? Cuz if it is, I can totally text my mom and ask to get my old phone back. She could call the phone store or something and see if they still have it. We were supposed to be BFFs forever. That's what the extra F is for — forever. Well, maybe your forever is shorter than mine cuz we've only been BFFs for a week. I'll spit on this phone, too, if that helps. (*spits*) Pffft! See? Is that better? Are we BFFs again? What? You like Karen better? Is it cuz she has an iPhone and I don't? I'm gonna get my dad's old one when he's tired of it. So, I spit on my new phone for nothing? If it fogs up and my mom gets totally mad at me, I'm blaming it on you! Hey, I have an idea! Why don't I become BFFs with Jody who's BFFs with Stacy who was BFFs with Karen last week? So we can all be BFFs! Cool, right? Really? You mean it? Spit on it? (*Holds out her phone.*)

BLIND LINE DRAWING

Male/Female Dramatic
Age Range: 8 – 12
1.5 minutes   By Talia Pura

Today in art class, Ms. Evan said we were going to do a blind line drawing. I didn't know what she meant. Were we going to find a blind person and draw a line across his face? Maybe she meant that we'd put on blindfolds and then draw. That would be a disaster. Well, it turns out a blind line drawing is when you look at what you are drawing, but don't look at the page. That is way harder to do than you think it is. It's almost impossible not to look at the paper! I had to have Melissa hold a folder in front of me, between my eyes and my paper. It took five tries before I stopped glancing down at the folder. Also, you never take your pencil off the paper. You just go back and forth and all around, trying to draw the object. I was drawing a stapler. But hey, you know what? It wasn't bad, and it felt kind of good, because you didn't have to care what it looked like. It was funny, and turned out way better than some drawings I've really tried my best on. Sometimes you just have to let yourself go and not worry about how something will turn out.

BUBBLES

Male/Female Comedic
Age Range: 6 – 11
1 minute   By Joyce Storey

My dad can hold his breath a lot longer than me. And I can blow bubbles under water. I really can. I practice, like, a lot. Like, way a lot. Like, tons and tons and it's really fun. But sometimes if I don't do it right, they go up my nose and that makes it itchy but I learned not to scratch it until after I come up for air. Know why? Cuz then water goes up my nose, too, and it's really gross and yucky and my nose gets runny and I don't like it. But I like the bubbles. I'm learning to make, like, a motorboat sound with my mouth and I keep my nose above water and I get lots of bubbles. Can you make bubbles? Can your dad hold his breath way long under water? No? See, that's why my dad is the coolest dad ever! He taught me everything I know.

BULLIES

Male/Female Dramatic
Age Range: 6 – 14
1.5 minutes   By Talia Pura

I didn't know what to do! I knew I should be doing
something, but, I don't know, I guess I didn't want to
get hurt, and really, I didn't know if I could have made
a difference anyway. Look, it's not the first time I saw
someone get bullied on the playground and I'm sure it
won't be the last. I've actually been bullied, too. Kids
that are big for their ages are sometimes like that. Just
'cause they are bigger than you, they think they can
push you around, and let's face it, what are you going
to do about it if they do? Sometimes there is an adult
watching and they smarten up, but sometimes there
isn't. So, there I was, minding my own business, when
this big kid starts pushing around this kid way smaller
than me. I started to tell him to cut it out, but he turned
on me and I got scared. Luckily, that gave the little
kid just enough time to run away. Does that count as
helping? I don't know, 'cause I was too busy running
away myself to figure it out. I just know that if I were
big for my age, I would never do that to somebody else.

BUNNY NIGHT LIGHT

Male/Female Dramatic
Age Range: 6 – 10
1 minute   By Talia Pura

I'm not afraid of the dark. Really, I'm not. Okay, maybe I was a bit afraid of the dark when I was a little kid, but that was a long time ago. You don't have to be afraid of the dark to want to keep a night light on when you sleep. I just happen to like that bunny shaped night-light in my room. What's wrong with that? It was a gift from my auntie when I was little and it's cute. I like to look at it before I fall asleep, you know? I like its funny little ears and nose. The fact that it also means my room doesn't get completely dark is beside the point. So, don't mess with my bunny.

BUNNY PRESENT

Male/Female Comedic
Age Range: 6 – 10
2 minutes   By Joyce Storey

Um, Mrs. Thompson, I have a very important question to ask you about your daughter's birthday present. Umm, it's very important. Did I say that already? See, here's the thing...can I buy her a bunny? I know you already have a hamster and a couple of cats and whatever that other thing in the cage is, but Skyler really needs a bunny. So can I? Please? Can I buy her a bunny? I know she'd really love it and my mom said I can if you say okay. So, it's totally up to you. See, my mom won't let me get one of my own but if I give it to Skyler I can come and play with it everyday. And we have lots of carrots in our garden that I can bring over to feed it. And we'll name him Squiggy. I think I'll get a boy, unless you want a girl, but then girls have babies, which would be nice if you want more. It would be fun to have a whole pile of bunnies! We could dress them up on Easter! And teach them how to lay chocolate eggs and everything! Maybe we'll name the mother Rosemary after my grandma. She'd like that. And Skyler can help me pick the names for the babies. So what do you think? Can I? Pleeeease? It'll be the best gift ever! Skyler will be so excited! You don't want to disappoint two children, do you, Mrs. Thompson?

CANDY CRUSH RUSH

Male Comedic
Age Range: 7-14
2 minutes   By Joyce Storey

Whoa! That was the coolest thing ever! When you get two of those chocolate covered ones with sprinkles, it clears everything! Wow! That was so awesome. I beat the level and everything. Mom, you just don't understand. I've been working on this level for weeks. I'm so sick of clearing the jelly and now I finally did it! Now I know why they call it "Candy Crush." I absolutely crushed it! What a rush! No, I am not obsessed with sugar. I do not need to see a nutritionist. I beat the level! This is the greatest accomplishment of my life! You should be rewarding me! ...I don't think having me do household chores is a reward. I was thinking more like buying me a bike or a new app or something. There are some very educational apps these days. Candy Crush is highly educational. I learn spatial reference and pattern mapping — is that a term? Like, if I make an L-shape with one color, I make a flat one and then if I get four in a row it goes striped and then I have to figure out how to get those two together so they can make exploding striped ones. And that's awesome! See, it's complicated problem solving. I should get a credit for it. I think I'll ask my math teacher about that. Oh, and the guy always says "sweet" when I do well. And that's good for my self-esteem. See? I'm not wasting my time at all. Now how about that bike?

CAR TALKS

Male/Female Dramatic
Age Range: 9 – 12
1.5 minutes   By Talia Pura

I am starting to miss being a little kid, sitting in a booster seat behind my mom when she drives. Lately, she's decided that driving anywhere is the perfect time to talk. She wants to know how I FEEL about things. Usually, it's things that I don't really want to talk about. If she asked me about that stuff when we were home, I'd just make up an excuse to leave the room, like I had to use the bathroom or something. But when you're in the front seat of the car, you're trapped. There is nowhere to go. She's got you right up until you get home, which can be a very long time. She tries to be all casual about it, but I always know what's coming when she does this really long drawn out, "soooo." That is becoming my least favorite sound in the world. She asks me a question, and waits. She won't take mumbling for an answer, either. But, what can I do? I still need rides to my friends' houses and after school activities. There's no bus route out to my house and it's still years before I can get my license. I'm trapped! There's nothing I can do but talk!

CHICK-FIL-A

Male/Female Comedic
Age Range: 12 – 16
2 minutes By Joyce Storey

Mom, I'm looking for money for Chick-fil-A. Where can I find some? I know I have my allowance, but this is food. Isn't it the parents' responsibility to provide food and shelter for their kids? You're the ones who brought us into the world in the first place. You should have realized we'd want to go to Chick-fil-A. Don't they teach you that in parent school? It's the first thing I'd put on the curriculum. Well, right after time to play Wii. I know you're cooking tonight but I have basketball practice. Besides, everyone on the team is going to Chick-fil-A. I need my social time. It's a very important part of my evolution as a teenager. Trust me, you don't want me growing up to be a dweeb. Well, Dad is a bit of one, but I think that automatically happens when you turn forty. Anyway, I'm saving my allowance for other stuff. Lots of stuff, like accessories for my iPad. They have some really cool speakers that I want. I know money doesn't grow on trees. That's why I get an allowance, right? But I don't think it should have to include Chick-fil-A. Don't they have a rulebook about that or something? They should. If I have to start paying for stuff like that, then I think we need to renegotiate my contract. Don't I get a cost of living increase or something? Ask Dad what the inflation rate is this year. He's good at math. He'll probably be able to figure it out. Unless, of course, you just want to pay for Chick-fil-A and call it a day? So where can I find some money? How about your wallet? That's a good place to look, don't you think? A twenty would be nice.

COOL HOTEL

Male/Female Comedic
Age Range: 5 – 10
1 minute   By Joyce Storey

Mom, this hotel is super amazing! Do you think they have a bathroom here? I need to go to the bathroom. Actually, I need to go pretty bad. See? I'm doing the dance. I can't help it! Do you think anyone's looking? Can I hide behind you? Do you think they'll know why I'm dancing? Or will they just think I'm artistic? Can't Dad check in faster? Mom, I really need to go. How come you don't dance around when you have to go? Do you ever have to go bad, Mom? Or is that a kid thing? Does Dad ever have to go when he's in a meeting? Do you call him and remind him to go? You know, like you do before we get in the car? Mom, I'm serious. This hotel is way cool but it'll be cooler if it has a bathroom, RIGHT NOW!

DANCING ENTREPRENEUR

Female Comedic
Age Range: 8 – 11
2 minutes   By Joyce Storey

I can read, eat and dance at the same time. Do I get extra allowance for that? You gave extra to Jason just for getting his homework done by 9:00. And he didn't even get all the answers right. He's not very good at math. Maybe you should get him a tutor or something. And he only did one thing. I'm doing three. I know it's not homework or anything, but it could be. I could be reading my story from Mrs. Mills' class if I wanted to. It's just so boring. Why do I want to read about some old guy who invented a light bulb when all he had to do was buy one at Wal-Mart? And now they have those curly ones. Did you know you can save money on your electric bill with them? That's what Mrs. Mills says. Do you think she's right? Probably. She's always right. She wouldn't like it if I read school stuff while I eat and dance cuz I might get PB&J on my schoolbook, right? And that would be bad. It's better if I just read my texts. I got one from Jenna. She's at her Dad's house this weekend. Can I go over? They're going bowling. Hey, I bet I can text back while I dance. Wanna see? That's why texting's great, cuz you don't have to talk with your mouth full. I wonder if I can drink and dance at the same time. The peanut butter gets stuck on the roof of my mouth. I could drink milk and if I spill it, it's okay cuz mommies always say, "Don't cry over spilt milk!" Ha! I could tell jokes while I eat, drink, read, text, and dance. That's gotta be worth extra allowance. What about it, Mom?

DISHES LEAD TO TATTOOS!

Female Comedic
Age Range: 6 – 13
2 minutes   By Joyce Storey

Why do I have to do the dishes? It's not even my night. Isn't Billy on trash? Well, dishes can be trash, can't they? If they're paper? Why don't we use paper dishes? Is that bad for the environment? It works for McDonald's. They wouldn't do anything bad for the environment, would they? If we had paper dishes, then Billy could take them all out with the trash and I could do fun stuff. You know, like singing Taylor Swift songs or listening to Taylor Swift or watching Taylor Swift's concert on YouTube! I bet Taylor Swift's Mom doesn't make her do dishes. She gets to wear pretty dresses and cool hair and get tattoos on her arms. If I do the dishes, can I get a tattoo? I want one like Taylor Swift has! Wow! That would be awesome! How many dishes do I have to do to make enough allowance to get a Taylor Swift tattoo? Does she have real tattoos or does she just write on her arms for concerts? I bet if I got a tattoo like her, I could get famous and ride around on a tour bus and everything! Come to think of it, maybe dishes aren't so bad after all. If I got a quarter for every dish, I could make a fortune! Mom, you have to raise my allowance. At this rate, I'll be like a hundred before I make enough money to be famous. How old do you have to be to get a tattoo, anyway? What? There's blood involved? And pain? Well, that's crazy pants! Who would do that? Can't I just get the kind you lick and put on your arm? You can get them free with certain kinds of gum. And then I wouldn't have to do dishes to pay for them. Mom, seriously, I don't have time for dishes. I have to go find some fake tattoos! I'm practically a celebrity!

DIVORCE

Male/Female Dramatic
Age Range: 9 – 15
1 minute   By Talia Pura

So, here's the thing. I don't actually know how I feel about my parents getting a divorce. Do I wish that my mom and dad still lived together? Well, yeah, I guess so. Isn't that what every kid is supposed to want? It's a pain packing up my stuff and going over to my dad's house every other weekend. I love my dad, and I'm sorry that I don't get to see him more. And I love my mom, too. I want them to be happy, and let's face it: They were not happy living together. Every day, I'd wonder if it was going to be a yelling kind of day, or a nobody-is-going-to-say-a-single-word-to-each-other kind of day. I used to wish they could just be nice to each other. Didn't they love each other when they got married, and when they had me? I've seen the pictures. They were smiling. What went wrong?

DRAW MY FAMILY

Male/Female Dramatic
Age Range: 6 – 11
1 minute   By Talia Pura

Draw my family. You want me to draw my family? Why? Shouldn't we just draw anything we want to draw? Maybe I feel like drawing a flower today, or a spaceship, or maybe I want to draw the whole universe. You always want all the pictures up on the wall of the classroom to look the same. I used to draw my family all the time. Our fridge is covered in pictures of my family, but you know what? My dog isn't in the picture anymore, and I don't want to draw a picture of my family without her in it. My sister wants to get another puppy right away, but I'm not ready for that. I miss Trixie and a new puppy isn't going to change that. So, I'm going to draw a picture of Trixie catching her ball, like she used to do. Let's put that picture up on the wall today.

DRAWING CLASS

Male/Female Dramatic
Age Range: 6 – 12
1 minute   By Talia Pura

My mom put me in an after-school arts program. I've
always loved to draw, ever since I can remember. So,
instead of just letting me do it, I have to go to a class for
it, now. I figured it might be okay when I got there and
saw drawings of coats on hangers that looked so real. I
thought, cool, I want to learn how to do that. But, then
the teacher told us we were all going to draw a circus
from our imaginations, after she played some stupid
circus music. I told her I wanted to draw like the stuff
up on the walls. She said that was just for the older
kids with more experience, and we were all going to
start with a circus. I don't want to go back, but Mom
thinks my circus elephants look great, so I have to go
again. Great, but until then, I'm going to try drawing
the clothes hanging in my closet.

DUMB BOYS

Female Comedic
Age Range: 11 – 16
2 minutes   By Joyce Storey

My boyfriend and your boyfriend are *not* the same at all! Just because he cheated on me with Jenny doesn't make him a jerk. Well, he *is* a jerk for doing it but he's really, really sorry and it was her who tricked him into it and he's a dumb guy so it wasn't really his fault. Not like your guy. He has cheated on you like, three times already. He did so! With Jenny first. I KNOW! Can you believe that Jenny? She's got some nerve! I mean, why doesn't she get her own boyfriend? She's always stealing ours. How can you even talk to her? It's her fault. It's not their fault they're too dumb to know how sneaky she is. Well, your guy's as dumb as a box of rocks; my guy is just dumb. Actually, they're both pretty dumb. I guess they *are* the same. I mean, if they like Jenny, they must be dumb, right? OMG! Do you think that makes us dumb? Because my parents would be really upset if I were dumb! Do you think Jenny thinks I'm dumb? I know she thinks *you're* dumb! Oh, I didn't mean that in a bad way. She just thinks you're dumb for staying with your boyfriend. She told me. Well, of course, I talk to her. Who do you think helps me with my homework? But I'm not talking to her this week because she cheated on me with my dumb boyfriend. Come to think of it, I don't like my dumb guy anymore. Let's break up with them both and be smart. Wanna?

EASTER EGGS

Female Comedic
Age Range: 6 – 11
1.5 minutes   By Joyce Storey

I have an Easter egg hunt today. I can't wait! Molly
and Max are coming. I wish it was just Molly but her
mom said she could only go if Maxie came too. Which
is a real drag, cuz I know he's gonna break everyone's
eggs. I just know it. Why do boys always have to
smash everything? Once I found this cool cobweb and
I showed it to my cousin Frankie and the first thing
he did was hit it with a stick. What is it with boys and
sticks? They think everything is a weapon. My mom
says it's a phase every four-year-old goes through but
I think they have something wrong with their brains.
Anyways, Molly is really fun to hunt Easter eggs with.
Last year, we collected more than anyone and we won
a prize — which was more Easter eggs. We ran out of
room in our baskets and they overflowed and Frankie
ran around smashing them. So I guess we all had fun
but I can't wait till he grows out of his "phase." Maybe
I'll hit him over the head with a stick and see how *he*
likes it.

FINAL FOUR

Male Dramatic
Age Range: 9 – 16
2 minutes   By Joyce Storey

Well, obviously, you're not getting it cuz you're
laughing like it's a big joke or something. This is no
joke. If I fail this test, I fail math — and if I fail math, I
fail the year. And if I fail the year, I'm grounded for life!
I hate math. I just don't get it, you know? My brain gets
all mixed up and all the numbers look the same. The
teacher might as well speak some other language. Or
maybe she already does and I didn't notice cuz I'm so
confused. My mom is going to be so mad at me. And
Dad? Forget it. I won't be going to another game with
him for like a hundred years after this. And wouldn't
you know, it's the Final Four this weekend. Final
Four. You know, basketball. March Madness? College
playoffs? Don't you know anything? It's like the most
important weekend in college basketball. You start
with all the teams and the losers get eliminated each
game. The winners move on until you get to the Final
Four. It's a really big deal and my dad's bracket is doing
fantastic and we were going to go to our friend's house
and watch the games together. Now, that's all ruined...
What do you mean? That's got nothing to do with
math... It does? You're joking. Really? You add up the
losers and subtract the winners and that's the answer?
No way! It's that easy? Then why did the teacher go
on and on? Some problem about, "If a train's going
60 miles an hour and it passes another train..." I can't

remember the rest. Why didn't she just say what you said? So if I subtract the winners from the losers, can I answer the test questions? I can? No kidding? Really, no joke? ...Wooooow. You're the most awesome tutor ever! (*pause*) But you gotta start liking basketball.

FIRST KISS

Female Comedic
Age Range: 11 – 15
1.5 minutes   By Talia Pura

It's cool how when you kiss someone, everything
works out so perfectly. Even when you've never kissed
anyone before, and you weren't expecting the kiss
to happen. You're just hanging around, thinking that
he's just going to keep talking and never get around to
actually kissing you. And then, when you least expect
it, he gives you that look, and you look back at him, and
you just know it's going to happen. He sort of leans
in toward you, so you lean in, too, and instead of just
bumping into his nose or something, it all just works
out perfectly. Your mouths open at precisely the right
time and your lips fit together like puzzle pieces. It's
strange to think how Zach's mouth fit together with
mine. He wanted to kiss me. I could tell. Before I'd ever
been kissed, I thought that I'd remember every single
moment, every movement of that very first one. But
when the time actually came, it was all sort of a blur,
and now, I can't remember anything about it, except
that it was really good, and I felt like my head was kind
of spinning. And then he ended it with a sloppy peck
on the corner of my mouth that left his spit behind,
and it got all crusty afterward. It sounds disgusting,
but it isn't, because it's Zach's spit. Isn't that just too
romantic? Couldn't you just die?

FISH ELMO

Male/Female Comedic
Age Range: 5 – 8
1.5 minutes   By Joyce Storey

Mommy, look at this big one! He likes me! He came right up to me. Look at his cute nose. Oh, let's look at other interesting fish. (*Shrieks*) Ahh! Mommy, I didn't know that was you behind me! You almost made me think a fish jumped right out of the water. Wouldn't that be fun? If he jumped all the way up into my arms and said, "Hello"?! I would name him Elmer. That's a good fish name; don't you think? Or is it too old fashioned? What about Elmo like on *Sesame Street?* The fish is red just like Elmo and I bet he's sweet, too. Do you think we could take him home? That would be fun! I'd tell him bedtime stories and tuck him in. Do you think he likes flannel sheets? I don't want him to catch cold. What? You mean, he has to stay in water ALL the time? Can't he just come out once in a while and play tag or hide-and-seek or something? It must get boring swimming around in a circle all the time. I'm glad he has a big pond at least, so he can go exploring. Can I take swimming lessons so I can go on adventures with Elmo? How long do you think it'll take me to get good? Maybe we'll find a secret cave or something. Or we can have a jumping contest or see who can hold their breath the longest. We're going to have so much fun! Mom, come on! We have to go buy a swimsuit — now!

GENIUS

Male/Female Comedic
Age Range: 10 – 15
2 minutes   By Joyce Storey

I just finished my math homework in like half an hour.
That was the most productive half hour of my life! I
should quit math. I'm a genius! I must be a genius if I
finished so fast, right? Why do I need math? Or the rest
of school, for that matter? Geniuses don't need school,
do they? Why would they, if they know everything
already? I talked to one of the geniuses at the Mac Store
the other day. I asked him if he was born a genius of if
he became one. He said he became one from helping
his mom with her computer problems. Well, I help my
mom, too. And not just with computer stuff. Sometimes
I load the dishwasher for her. She gives me a dollar to
do it, but still... That must make me a double genius!
Maybe I can work at the Mac Store once I quit school.
I'm gonna have lots of spare time on my hands, so I
might as well work. Mind you, they work at a genius
bar. Don't you have to be at least 21 to work at a bar?
Maybe I could lie about my age. I wouldn't want to fake
my ID though, cuz I could get into trouble. Isn't that
like a felony or something? I'll have to Google it and
find out. Some genius I'd be if I landed in jail. I wonder
if they have geniuses in jail? They probably do, cuz
someone has to mastermind the bank robbery, right? It
probably wasn't the genius' fault that they got caught.
He probably had everything worked out, but I bet there
was this dumb guy who tripped the alarm. The genius

probably told him not to do that but he didn't listen. He shoulda hired better guys. Maybe being a genius isn't all it's cracked up to be... I don't want to be playing basketball in prison. I think I'll go to school tomorrow after all.

GETTING A DOG

Male/Female Dramatic
Age Range: 6 – 12
1 minute   By Talia Pura

We're getting a dog. We're actually getting a dog! My brother and I have been begging for a dog for ages, but our parents always said no. Mom was sure that we would never remember to feed it. My dad thought he'd get stuck walking it. So, my brother and I made up a presentation and showed it to them on Saturday morning. We made posters with pictures and all the reasons that we wanted a dog. Instead of just begging, we convinced them with logic. Besides teaching us responsibilities, because we are totally going to be the ones taking care of it, we said it would teach us more about love. I saw my mom tear up a little when I said that. I think that's what got her. So, now we get to choose a rescue dog. I can hardly wait to see which dog we'll bring home and love forever.

GIANT REDWOODS

Male/Female Dramatic
Age Range: 9 – 15
1 minute   By Talia Pura

Wow, this is amazing! Just look at this! This is the coolest thing ever. When I was a little kid, my mom read me a story about the Redwood Forest, and I've wanted to come here ever since. Some of the trees here are so big, even when my mom and dad and brother and I all try to put our arms around one, our fingers don't touch! Redwoods are the tallest trees in the world. I can't believe that any tree can be so tall, or so old. Some of them are almost 3,000 years old. That's when the first people came here. I could be looking at the same tree that they looked at. And the forests were here even before that. That's hard to think about, how these trees could be here when there wasn't anyone here to look at them. I'll bet they'll be here forever, too. Some things don't need people at all.

GIRLFRIEND

Male Comedic/Dramatic
Age Range: 7 – 14
2 minutes   By Joyce Storey

I don't like that she doesn't answer texts. Do you think that means she doesn't like me? Girls are hard. They giggle all the time and you think they're making fun of you but then your friend tells you that one of them told him the friend of the other one likes you and that's why she's giggling. How am I supposed to know that? But Jason said she said her friend said she thought I was cool. Do you think I'm cool, Mom? Are skateboards and drones and video games cool? Do girls like that stuff? I mean, Sarah must or she wouldn't giggle, right? I'm practicing this flip with my board and I'm gonna do it in front of her but I gotta practice more cuz if I wipe out when she's watching, I will just die cuz I won't ever be able to look at her again. It's been like 13 minutes and she still hasn't answered my text. Do you think she's mad or something? Do you think it was my text? I said, "What's up?" That's good, right? Like, "What's up? Why do you just giggle all the time and why won't you talk to me in school and why did you smile in gym class and why does your hair shine in the sun and why do you always wear a headband and why are you so smart in math and why haven't you answered my text?!" Honestly, Mom, I can't take it. This not knowing is driving me nuts. That's it — I'm breaking up with her. I'll send a text. (*Looks at phone*) OMG, that's her! She texted back! (*Reading*) "Hey." Mom, she texted

"Hey." She does like me! Oh, this is an emotional roller coaster. What should I say now? I've already used up my best line. Whoa, I think I'm getting dizzy. I gotta lay down and think!

GO PLAY OUTSIDE

Male/Female Comedic
Age Range: 6 – 12
1 minute   By Talia Pura

"Go play outside." My mom says that to me every single day when I get home from school. "When I was your age, my mom didn't let me sit on the sofa and stare at a screen for hours, and you can't either." Argh! Why does she always compare me with herself when she was my age? Maybe kids in the olden days liked to go play outside. My friends and I don't, okay? Playing outside is boring. What are we supposed to do outside anyway? Okay, yes, we could go to the park. And yes, I know that we have a basketball hoop on the driveway. We played basketball last week. We don't need to play it again today. Wait, what's that? Wow, a new bike. I got to go, my friend is outside. I've got to see that new bike!

GOBLIN IN MY CLOSET

Male/Female Comedic
Age Range: 6 – 10
1 minute   By Joyce Storey

Do you think goblins are real? Tommy said there's a goblin in my closet and it's going to eat me unless I do his chores for a week. And that made me scared — not the part about the chores; I mean the goblin. But I pretended it didn't. But then I got thinking, how come it didn't eat Tommy? Because *he* hasn't done his chores in two weeks. And does it only eat bad kids? Are there any vegetarian goblins? They don't eat people, right? I cleaned my closet three times but I didn't find the goblin. Do you think maybe he went out for coffee or a job or something? I wish I could see him. Just for a second. He would be great at show-and-tell. Do you think he would come to school with me for one day? It would be worth doing Tommy's chores for a week just for that!

GOLDFISH

Male/Female Comedic
Age Range: 6 – 11
1.5 minutes   By Joyce Storey

Would you like a Goldfish®? They're my favorite snack.
You can have more than one. I can take them out of the
bag for you if you want. When you lay them out on the
table, they look like a whole school of fish swimming
up the stream. Or do they swim down the stream?
I'm not sure. I think it depends on the fish. I think
salmon swim upstream. Do you like salmon? I think my
Goldfish taste better but Mom says salmon is good for
me. How come everything that tastes bad is good for
you? Fish is fish. I don't know why my Goldfish aren't
as good as smelly old salmon. They have all kinds of
flavors of Goldfish, too. Like saltine and pretzel and
flavor blasted. They even have colors, which doesn't
make sense to me cuz they're called «gold» fish, not
green fish or red fish or any other colored fish. If
they're goldfish, they should just be gold, right? Not
that I wouldn't eat them. They're all pretty good but
I like cheddar the best. They really hit the spot in my
stomach! Do you have a favorite? You kinda look like an
animal cracker guy to me.

GRAFFITI

Male/Female Dramatic
Age Range: 6 – 12
1 minute   By Talia Pura

I wrote my name on the bathroom wall. I was really
little, and had just learned how to write my own name.
Of course, my mom found it, and asked if I had done it.
I told her a lie and said it wasn't me. It really couldn't
have been anyone but me. But it felt so good! I started
to write it everywhere, until my mom taught me about
graffiti. We took a drive and she showed me all the
places people write their names, and usually, it makes
a big mess on the walls. But then she took me to an art
center that's filled with graffiti, on purpose. It was the
coolest place ever! She helped me figure out different
ways of writing my name, but made me promise to only
write it on paper. I guess that's okay, for now, but one
day I want my graffiti to hang in that art gallery.

GRANDMA'S COOKIES

Male/Female Dramatic
Age Range: 6 – 12
1 minute   By Talia Pura

My grandma makes the best cookies. Every time I go
to her house, I eat at least one, maybe two or three.
They are oatmeal chocolate chip cookies. I feel pretty
bad for kids who don't have grandmas who bake them
cookies. Getting a cookie out of a package someone
brought home from the store is just not the same
thing. I guess it's still a cookie, but my grandma's
chocolate chip cookies are a whole different kind
of treat. Yesterday, she came over to my house and
stayed with me because I had a cold and couldn't go
to school. She brought me a new book to read. She sat
beside my bed and read it to me. But first, she gave
me a cookie. It can't be a bad day when I get one of my
grandma's cookies.

GREEN EYES

Female Comedic/Dramatic
Age Range: 7 – 11
2 minutes   By Joyce Storey

Mom, why didn't you give me green eyes? I want green eyes! Brown eyes don't look good. They don't match anything I wear! Can you take them back for another color? Cats have green eyes. I like cats. Can you give me cat eyes? They're a cool shape. Can you change the shape? But I don't want slits on my pupils. It looks pretty cool on Fluffy, but I think that would look creepy on people, don't you? I don't want to look creepy. That's totally not what I'm going for. I have enough problems without that. I want to be cute like my friend, Linda. She's super cute. Well, I guess she is. I mean, I don't know for sure, but all the boys say that about her. I heard Javi talking in the library when he wasn't supposed to. He was telling Lucas how cute she was. They didn't know I was listening. Do you think they ever say that about me? I doubt it because I have brown eyes. Brown eyes are boring. Everybody has brown eyes. What's so special about that? Why didn't you think of green eyes when you were making me? I mean, didn't you even give it any thought? Did you talk it over with Dad or did he just decide? You can't leave these things to boys, Mom. They don't have good taste. Well, I guess some of them do cuz they think Linda is cute, so they must know. But I don't think Dad is that kind of guy. I mean, he's color-blind, isn't he?

Is that why his shirt never matches anything else he's wearing? Honestly, Mom, I don't know what you were thinking. You should never let a man do a woman's work. Now I have to live with the consequences.

HE TOOK MY STUFF!

Female Comedic
Age Range: 6 – 9
2 minutes   By Joyce Storey

Mommy, he took my water! My bucket was full and
he poured it out! I don't care that I wasn't using it!
It's mine! I was busy doing other things but I planned
to come back to it. And even if I don't, it's still mine.
He just wants to wreck things all the time. How am I
supposed to have time to be a princess and walk around
with my face painted in my pretty dress when I have to
watch my little brother? It's not fair! He doesn't have
to watch me! I know he's only four, but when I was
four, I STILL had to watch him! I mean, I think I did…
I don't really remember cuz I was only four, but I bet I
did! I mean, he was barely born then, so he probably
didn't take my stuff as much, but I bet he did when you
weren't looking! Did you ever think of that? I bet that's
what happened to all those things I lost. You know,
that sweater that you asked me if I left at school? I bet
Wyatt took it! He probably did! And those keys that
you lent me to play with that time that went missing? I
bet he took them! Did you ever think of that, huh? We
have a criminal living under our roof and you didn't
even notice it! That's why I'm going to be a detective
when I grow up, cuz I'm smart, and I want to be just like
Detective Beckett on "Castle," that show you watch, cuz
she's pretty and I bet she wore a princess dress when
she was young like me and… There he goes again! Now
he's using my shovel for a sword. Why can't we go to the
beach with girls? I need more handmaidens!

HOMEWORK

Male Comedic
Age Range: 10-15
1.5 minutes   By Joyce Storey

I hate homework! I spend my whole day doing schoolwork. Why do I have to do more when I get home? I have stuff to do, ya know. I have to check my Facebook page and text my friends. And there's basketball practice and hanging with my peeps. My buddy, Josh is havin' a bunch of us over to play Wii. I'm defending my championship in both bowling and golf. What am I supposed to tell him, I can't, cuz I have homework? I don't think so. Well, not unless Mom finds out. She'll get all mad and stuff if I don't do it… I guess I could actually do it before I go to Josh's house. It'll probably only take an hour. And we're getting out early today anyway cuz of some PTA meeting. And it's really not that hard. I kinda like math. I'm pretty good at it, actually. I know the answer to the first question already. I was looking at it on the bus ride home. Okay, I'll do it early this one time. Mom'll die of shock when I tell her it's done and she doesn't have to nag me about it. Come to think of it, it'll be fun just to see the look on her face! I better get started. I can't wait till she gets home!

I DON'T LIKE TOMATOES!

Male/Female Comedic
Age Range: 6 – 12
2 minutes   By Joyce Storey

I don't like tomatoes! They're gross. I don't care if
they're good for me — they're yucky! Like really, really
yucky. They're all runny and stuff and they have seeds
and I don't like seeds. Well, maybe I do. I don't know
about that part for sure cuz you can't taste the seeds
cuz of the yuck around them. I don't get why Mom
always wants me to eat stuff that's good for me. Why
can't it just be stuff I like? You know, like pizza and
stuff. Come on, Waldo, you gotta help me out here.
Eat 'em up before she comes back and makes me try
to swallow them. What kind of dog are you, anyway?
You're supposed to eat everything that moves. I bet
if it were cat food you'd eat it. You love cat food more
than the cats. I sure can't eat 'em — not the cat food,
tomatoes. They make me gag and if I gag, I could choke
and if I choke, I could go to the hospital and stuff. And
that would be awful. My sister was in the hospital
when she had her tonsils out. Remember? They fed her
ice cream. But they never gave her tomatoes. Not one
tomato, but they gave her all the ice cream she wanted.
It was pretty cool. Wait, hold on. I loooove ice cream!
Maybe it's worth a trip to the hospital. I never thought
of that before! Stop drooling on my tomatoes, Waldo.
They're already slimy enough and now I gotta try to
swallow 'em so Mom can call 911.

I HATE SLEEPOVERS

Male/Female Comedic
Age Range: 6 – 12
1.5 minutes   By Talia Pura

I hate sleepovers. I know that isn't normal. All kids love sleepovers, right? What's not to love about going over to a friend's house for the night and sleeping on a hard floor with a blanket that's too thin and a pillow that you can't punch down enough, and having someone else's dog come and slobber on your face early in the morning, just after you finally fall asleep? And why wouldn't I want to eat some other mom's idea of a good breakfast, with burnt toast and the wrong kind of jam and no peanut butter in sight? And how great is it to have your friend tell you the same ghost stories you've heard a million times when all you want to do is close your eyes and try to fall asleep — even though your friend's house has all these weird noises that your house doesn't have, and it smells funny from something your mom has never cooked for supper. What's not to love? Well, I'd tell you, but I'm too tired. Now, if you'll excuse me, I have to go curl up in my own bed, with my own dog, and my own blanket and perfect pillow. (*Big yawn*) Just tell my mom that I want some pancakes to eat when I finally wake up.

I WANT A PHONE

Male/Female Dramatic
Age Range: 8 – 12
1.5 minutes   By Talia Pura

I want a phone. I don't think that is too much to ask.
EVERYONE in my class has a phone. I'm the only one
that doesn't have a phone to leave in the teacher's
basket before class. She doesn't let us keep phones at
our desks. She says they're too distracting. Everyone
puts a phone in the basket except me. I feel like such
a loser. My mom won't get me a phone. She told me
research says that holding a phone to your ear causes
brain tumors. When I pointed out that no one holds a
phone up to their ears anymore except old people, she
said that holding a phone in front of my face all day is
just as bad, because it will ruin my eyes, cause me to
bang into things, and make me forget how to talk to
people for real. Well, that's happening anyway, because
all of my friends are staring at their phones instead
of talking to me. The only way I can talk to them is if I
get a phone to message them on. My mom just doesn't
understand modern communication!

I'M NOT A PENGUIN!

Male Comedic
Age Range: 5 – 10
1 minute   By Joyce Storey

I'm not a penguin! You keep telling me to join the
pack, Mr. Evans and hug you and the whole class and
everyone, cuz that's how penguins stay warm. And
my toes are cold and my fingers are cold and my
nose is runny and it's freezing out here, but I'm not
a penguin! I don't have a white vest or flippers or
anything. And I think they're slimy. Who would want
to be that slippery? How can they hug? They probably
slide right off of each other into the ocean. Did you
ever think of that? And then what if they drown? I'm
not a very good swimmer. I tried to take class at the
Y. My mom made me go and my dad took me, but I
don't like getting my face wet. It makes me class-
tro-phobic. Like this class. I don't want to hug every
single person. Becky's okay, but Jimmy punched me
yesterday at recess! (*To Jimmy*) I'm still mad at you,
Jimmy. Why would I want to hug you? You're not a
penguin either!

IT'S SO EMBARRASSING!

Male/Female Dramatic
Age Range: 7 – 12
1 minute   By Talia Pura

My sister won't keep her clothes on. I know she is barely three years old, but I'm pretty sure that I kept my clothes on when I was three. I know that it's because she doesn't like to wear a wet bathing suit when she gets out of the pool, but why not make her put clothes on as soon as she gets out then? I swam when I was three years old. That didn't make me want to run around naked all day. The worst part is that it's my birthday party next week, and all my friends are coming over to swim in the pool. I made my mom promise that the little brat is going to wear a bathing suit for the whole party, and Mom said, "of course"— just like it's what Brianne does all the time. I don't think Mom even notices that she's always naked. It drives me nuts! She'd better keep her suit on, or I'll be so embarrassed!

IT'S TIME

Male/Female Dramatic
Age Range: 6 – 11
1 minute   By Talia Pura

I know you think you are doing me a favor, but
honestly, do you not think that I can do this myself? It
isn't that heavy and I know exactly where in my room
I want to put it. So please, just let me do it. ARGH! No,
really, thank you for the offer, but I'm not a little kid
anymore. Didn't I put my bike away just fine last night?
Didn't I sort out my laundry this morning? Right, so
why can't I decide where this goes in my room? You
want me to stay a little kid forever! I know you love me,
and I know I'm very cute, but, please! Let me grow up
already! From now on, I decide what I wear to school,
okay? And I decide when, and IF to get my hair cut,
and right now, I decide where to put this in my room.
Thank you. That's all I ask. For now.

LITTLE DUDE

Female Comedic
Age Range: 6 – 11
2 minutes   By Joyce Storey

I'm having a baby brother and I have three names for
him: Scooby-Doo, Little Dude and Cookie Monster. I'm
not sure which one I like best. Do you have to pick?
Could I call him, say, Scooby-Doo on Mondays and
Cookie Monster Tuesdays? He could be Little Dude on
the weekends, cuz that sounds really relaxed. Mom and
Dad are relaxed on the weekends. Me, too. I like them
cuz there's no school and stuff and we do fun things
like go to the park or the zoo or something. And I get
ice cream and fun snacks. Do you think Little Dude will
get ice cream, too? I hope I don't have to share mine
with him cuz I don't want his germs. Babies are all
drooly and gross. And they throw their food. I hope he
doesn't throw food in my hair or on my favorite top or
something. That would be totally horrible. My friend
Kadie has to share with her brother. He doesn't throw
his food or anything, but she still doesn't like it. So,
Little Dude'll just have to get his own ice cream. Dad'll
probably spoil him cuz he's a boy and boys like other
boys. But I don't mind, cuz Mom'll like me better, right?
I mean, she will, right? Or will she like him better cuz
I picked cool names for him? Maybe I better pick bad
ones for Wednesday, Thursday and Friday. That way
she's sure to like me the best at least three days a week.
I have to go now and think up more names.

LONG RANGE PLAN

Female Comedic
Age Range: 11 – 16
2 minutes   By Talia Pura

My boyfriend of five weeks — I know, right — we've
been going out forever! So, my boyfriend of five weeks
asked me what I thought we'd be doing after we
finished high school, and I said, "Do you think we'll still
be going out?" And he said, "Sure, why wouldn't we
be?" And I didn't know what to say, but now I've given
it some thought. I hope that he asks me that again,
because next time I'll have an answer all planned out.
We'll go to the same college, and then we'll get married
and go to Europe on our honeymoon — unless he wants
to go to Disney World or something, but I think Europe
would be romantic. And then we'll move to San Diego
and have three kids, named Julie May, Angela Katherine,
and Christine Sophia if they are girls, and if they are
boys, there'll be a Zach Jr., but he'll have to go by his
middle name so we can tell them apart. Then Ryan, with
no middle name because nothing goes with Ryan, and
Kyle Steven, with Steven spelled with a "v." Of course,
it's possible that some of these details will change. For
example, he could insist on Disney World, but I'd be
okay with that, too. It's always a good idea to have a
long-range plan in place. My mother is always telling me
to be prepared, and sometimes I find that really difficult
to do, so, I'm glad that's out of the way. I definitely feel
better now. It's one less thing to worry about.

LUCKY QUARTER

Male/Female Comedic
Age Range: 6 – 12
1.5 minutes   By Talia Pura

Oh, what's this? (*picks something up off the floor*) A quarter! I found a quarter. Wow, I never find money. My brother is always finding money on the sidewalk, but I never do. Wait till I tell him I found a quarter. All he ever finds is a penny, or maybe a nickel. I'm going to take this quarter and shove it in his face. He's always boasting about his stupid "lucky" pennies. Ha! And then I'm going to spend it on candy. I know 25 cents isn't very much, but it's free money, so that candy is going to taste really good! (*looks at the coin more closely*) Oh, wait a minute. This isn't a quarter. It's just a piece of metal — a slug, I think they call it. Why would anyone drop a slug on the sidewalk? Just to mess with me, I guess. (*sighs*) Well, that was nice while it lasted. But, I still found it, and since I can't spend it, I'm going to keep it in my pocket. I'll bet it's luckier than a penny.

MONSTER UNDER MY BED

Male/Female Comedic
Age Range: 7 – 12
2 minutes   By Talia Pura

Everyone knows that ghosts aren't real, but monsters, well, maybe they are, and maybe they aren't. When I was a little kid, I had one living under my bed. Finally, my mom got me a dog and Skippy kept him away until he moved out of our house forever. It's a good thing, because sharing my room with a monster was really tricky. I didn't usually think about him when I first went to bed. After brushing my teeth and getting my bedtime story, my mom would turn out the light, and I'd just fall asleep. But then, if I had to get up in the middle of the night to use the bathroom, I couldn't let my feet touch the floor. Touching the floor was the only actual way that the monster could bite or grab me. As long as I only stepped on my dirty jeans and T-shirts, I could make it to the door and back to my bed. My mom didn't understand that I HAD to leave my clothes lying all over my floor. The nights after laundry days were bad. Once, I had a huge meltdown after she didn't even leave me the clothes that I had just worn that day. They weren't even dirty enough to go in the laundry. That's when we started talking about getting Skippy. Thanks to him, I've kind of forgotten about the monster that used to live under my bed. Now I just have to deal with Skippy licking my face when it's too early to get up on Saturday mornings. That's a way better problem to have.

MY FAIRY

Female Dramatic
Age Range: 6 – 9
1 minute   By Joyce Storey

There's a fairy under my pillow. There really is! She doesn't talk or anything but I hear her wings flapping at night. Mom says it's just a fly cuz they make noise when they buzz around close to my light, but she doesn't know. Adults don't see fairies. Only kids. I talk to my fairy and she talks back. I say the words for her, but I know that's what's on her mind cuz she told me. Well, she didn't tell me, but I imagine what she would say and she says it. She's really pretty, too — all blue and green and glowy and she sparkles when I'm not looking. I named her Ariel cuz she reminds me of a princess. She saves me from monsters and no one can get me while I sleep. I don't care if you believe me or not! She's my friend and I like her!

MY PARENTS' ROOM

Female Dramatic
Age Range: 6 – 10
2 minutes   By Joyce Storey

I wish I didn't have to sleep in my parents' room. I mean, they don't make me or anything, but I always end up there. I have my own room down the hall. Mom calls it lavender but it's really purple. I got to redo it after my brother moved into a bigger room. And I have this way cool mural on the wall with ballerinas and mermaids and an awesome quilt on my bed with a picture of Ariel on it. She's so beautiful. I want to look like her when I grow up. And I have this giant dollhouse for my Barbies™ that my mom got me. Oh — and my lamp is really cool cuz my gran gave it to me. When it heats up, this lava stuff gets big and grows. She said she had one like it when she was a kid. So I love my room and I always start out sleeping in it. My dad reads me a bedtime story and my parents tuck me in, and everything's fine. But then in the middle of the night, I have these dreams and run into my parents' room. Sometimes I don't even remember doing it. I just wake up there. I feel kinda funny about it but Mom says she did the same thing when she was my age. She says I have an overactive imagination and the dreams won't hurt me. She said I should tell myself that I'm safe when I'm in the middle of them, but I never remember to, so I run to Mom and Dad instead. And then I never remember the dumb old dreams in the morning. I can't wait till next year when I'm big. Then I'm gonna punch my dreams in the nose, so I can stay in my own bed.

NEVER TELL A LIE

Male/Female Dramatic
Age Range: 8 – 14
1.5 minutes   By Talia Pura

My mom always says that I shouldn't tell a lie, but I don't think she really means it. Sure, if you do something wrong, you should admit it instead of blaming someone else, but I think there are some times when mom actually wants me to tell a lie. Like last week when my aunt was visiting. She came into the house and said, "Hello," to my mom and me. She'd gotten a new haircut, and it was just awful. My mom said she looked great, which was just not true. Then, she made me lie, too. She told my aunt she just knew I loved it. My aunt turned to face me and my mom glared at me behind her back. Of course, I had to lie and agree she looked great. That's not a big deal lie, just a fake compliment to make someone feel good. Then there are the kind of lies you tell to keep someone from freaking out, like, "Don't worry, that wasn't a spider on your shoulder just now, just a piece of lint," or "Your cat is going to come home again any day now; I just know it," even though you're pretty sure that kitty is gone forever. Sometimes, it's more important to help someone feel good than to tell the truth.

NO HAIR

Male/Female Comedic
Age Range: 6 – 11
1 minute   By Joyce Storey

Why you don't have any hair? You forget to water it?
My mama waters mine every day and puts shampoo on
it and I don't like it cuz it gets in my eyes. Mama says to
keep them closed but I always peek. What if something
happens and I miss it? What if a giant pterodactyl
flies in the window or an alien lands in the kitchen? I
wouldn't see it if I didn't peek. Do you peek? I guess not
or you woulda noticed somebody cutting off your hair.
What does it feel like being bald? Do you get cold in the
winter? I bet you get sunburnt up there. I can't see cuz
you're so tall. Hey, you know what would be cool? You
could draw a map of the world on there and then spin
in circles real fast like the real world! Wanna try? I got
markers! Let's start with Africa.

NO MORE SPARKLES

Female Comedic
Age Range: 7 – 12
1 minute   By Joyce Storey

Mom, you're going to have to face it sooner or later: I'm just not a girlie girl. I know you love that dress you bought me and I'm sorry that it was so expensive and all but, well, it has a lot of unnecessary sparkly things on it, don't you think? I just don't get sparkles. They don't do anything to hold the dress together and they're usually itchy. Did you ever have sparkles on the part that goes under your arms? They rub against you all the time and sometimes you get a rash. Then they fall off — the sparkles, not the rash — and they make things you touch sparkly. They're just annoying in general. What's wrong with T-shirts and tights? They're cute and I can still do flips when I want to. That's really important to consider when you buy clothes. You know — their flexibility? I've been working hard on my one-handed flip. How can I possibly do that in sparkles? I mean, really.

PARKING GUARD

Male/Female Comedic
Age Range: 7 – 11
2 minutes   By Joyce Storey

Mister, you can't park here! The ice cream truck will
be here any minute! If you park here he might not stop
and I've got money from my mom and I'm gonna get a
chocolate cone with sprinkles. I know you can't hear
him. That's cuz he's not here yet but I got a text from
Francine that he's on her block and he always comes
to our block next. Well, he's not actually at Francine's
block yet but he will be soon. She got a text from her
BFF Charlene that he's almost at her house and you
know he always goes to Francine's block after Charlene's
and then he'll be here and then it'll all be screwed up
if you're parked in his way. No, you can't just stay five
minutes! What if you get held up talking or something?
Adults always talk so much. What could you have to say
that would be more important than chocolate ice cream
with sprinkles? If I don't get my ice cream it will be your
fault and I'll grow up feeling sad for probably the rest of
my life and I'll have to go to therapy and the lady will ask
me why my life's ruined and I'll have to tell the truth and
say it's cuz this man wouldn't find a different parking
spot and then he talked too much and that wrecked my
chances of going to college because after that I couldn't
concentrate and I flunked out of school and it was
horrible! You wouldn't want that on your conscience
now, would you, Mister? Oh, and I forgot the part where
my parents go broke from all the shrink bills. So, make it
easy on yourself and find a different place to park, okay?

PATRICIA'S BIRTHDAY GIFT

Male Comedic
Age Range: 6 – 12
2 minutes   By Joyce Storey

Patricia is the one who gave me $60 and I'm keeping all of it. I'm going to invest in Google and make a bazillion dollars so I can save for college. Dad says that's about what college costs these days so I gotta start saving early cuz by the time I get there it'll probably be more like a zillion bazillion. I mean, I know my parents will save, too, and all but they're pretty old already. Dad is 32 and Mom is almost 30. Let's face it: Time is not on their side. By the time I'm that old I want to be set, ya know? Like set. I want a Lamborghini and a game room and a pool and a tennis court and a bunch more stuff. The most important thing is the game room. It'll be like a movie theater where I can play all my video games and have my friends over and kick their butts at *Ghost Recon Wildlands*. Do you think it'll still be popular by then? They're already on like the 10th one in the series, so by then they'll probably be on number 50 or something. I bet I'll still be really good. Do you think they'll still have Xbox and PlayStation in the future or should I hold off on buying them in case something cooler comes out? My game room's got to be the coolest thing on the planet. So, yeah, I'm saving Patricia's birthday gift so I can get into a good college and I can make zillions of dollars so I can whoop your butt at *Ghost Recon* number 50.

PENIS INFECTION

Male Comedic
Age Range: 6 – 12
1.5 minutes   By Joyce Storey

My dog has a penis infection. My mom says I'm not supposed to tell people but he does. She gives him a pill every day and we have to make sure he doesn't get dirty there. Just a sec... (*calls to mother*) "No one, Mom, just the postman." Sorry, did that offend you? I didn't mean that you're no one. Obviously, you're someone. You deliver the mail, after all. What's your name? Marvin? Is that like an old-timer name? I don't know any Marvins. Marvin Gaye? Who's he, your dad? No? Your uncle? (*pause while postman answers*) Oh. Why did your parents name you after a musician? I mean, it's cool and all, but why did they pick a dead one? I mean, I guess that's cool. I wasn't named after anyone. I'd like to be named after a sports star or a movie star or something but it'd have to be someone good. Dallas here was named after some cowboys. Not like "Home on the Range," but it's a whole team my dad likes. I think he likes his name okay. I mean Dallas, not my dad. He answers to it. And he seems happy except for his penis infection. That must be a drag. Don't tell Mom I told you. I think she thinks he's embarrassed about it or something, but I think he just wants to get better. What do you think?

POOP BAG

Male/Female Comedic
Age Range: 7 – 13
2 minutes   By Joyce Storey

Take a poop bag? Are you for real, Mom? Didn't he go today already? He shouldn't have to do everything AGAIN. That's just gross and I don't like that part. Can't he hold on till you take him out? Aw, Mom! Why can't dogs be toilet trained. I read that you can train cats. You just buy this kit for your toilet with a flag for the flusher and they learn to flush and everything. I'm gonna try it on T-Bone. If I use half my allowance can you pay the rest? Mom! I'm serious! You gotta help me out here! I don't like getting poop germs all over me! Of course, I don't touch it. Ew! What do you think I am, new? That's super gross! But I think the germs come through the bag anyway. This is child abuse! I could get some horrible disease! Ever think of that, huh? How come kids always have to walk their pets? Adults should do it. You're in charge of the family. I think it's your responsibility, Mom. Come on. Please? I'll clean my room twice this month. Promise. Okay, well, at least once and I'll do my homework. Oh, I forgot — I have a test! I have to go study! I need all the time I can to cram and keep my grades up and pass the year and get a good GPA so I can take AP classes and pass the SATs and get into a good college so I can get a good job and succeed in life! I don't have time to walk the dog. Sorry, Mom. Here's the leash. Make sure he steps off the curb when he pees!

PUPPY TALK

Female Comedic
Age Range: 6 – 12
2 minutes   By Joyce Storey

Mom, can we get a puppy? Can we name him after Dad? Do you think that would be confusing to have two Dads in the same house? I know you don't think I'll walk him, but I will, I swear I will. Larissa has two puppies. And she says they're no problem at all. Well, except that the new one, Morgan, pees on the rug a lot, but her Mom says that's normal. And he chewed her new sneakers, which made her Dad mad cuz he paid for them. And he ate the corner off the coffee table — not the Dad, the dog. But it's okay because he ate the opposite corner the next week, so now they match. And then the big puppy, who's actually a dog now, he accidentally stepped on the little one and broke his leg. Now little Morgan has a cute little pink cast. He looks adorable in his pictures! See? (*holds up cell phone*) And tomorrow after school, Larissa said I can come over and sign his cast if I want to and I really, really want to. So can I go, Mom? Please! Can I? It won't take long. And maybe I can get my picture taken with him for Facebook. Will you bring your phone, Mom, so I can get a picture? I know I'm not old enough for Facebook yet, but I can put it on Dad's site. How come you don't have a Facebook page, Mom? Larissa's Mom does, and she's pretty cool. So what do you think about the puppy? Can we get one with a cast? I bet they have them at the Humane Society. My teacher says you should always adopt a pet if you can instead of getting them at the pet store — cuz they come from puppy mills. Do puppies make flour? Larissa said that mills make flour. Is that right? I can't wait to go to Larissa's! What do you think I should wear? I think I'll wear pink to match the puppy. Do you think he'd like that? Mom? Are you listening? Mom?

SCIENTIFIC LAUGHTER

Male/Female Comedic
Age Range: 7 – 11
2 minutes   By Joyce Storey

I think I'm gonna do my science project on laughing.
I love to laugh, even when it gets me in trouble. I
giggled in math class the other day cuz Justin Murphy
was making cross-eyed faces at everyone in the back
seats. He cracks me up! He's sooooo funny. Anyways,
the teacher got mad at me cuz I giggled the loudest
of anyone. It was one of those great big belly laughs,
ya know? I couldn't help it! The guy's hysterical! And
I don't think the teacher was really mad cuz when I
couldn't stop laughing, she cracked up, too, and then
the whole class burst a gut. I was laughing so hard I
was crying and after a while no one even knew why we
were laughing. But the teacher said she felt better after
that and something about endorphins exploding in her
brain. Whoa! Now *that* made me real worried! I mean
it's a lot of responsibility on a kid to cause their teacher
to explode. So I went home that night and believe me,
I was quaking in my boots! How was I going to tell my
parents what I'd done? But I figured if I didn't fess up,
they'd probably get a call from the school tattling on
me and I'd be in worse trouble. What if my teacher
died or something? It was bedtime before I finally got
up the nerve to tell them. I thought they'd ground me
for a year but guess what? They laughed! They said
endorphins were good and they're scientifically proven
to increase their activity with laughter! Who knew?

That's when I got the idea for the science project. I figure every time I get caught in class for laughing I'll say it's part of my experiment. That oughta keep me out o' trouble for at least a month — as long as no more teachers explode.

SEASON OPENER

Male Dramatic
Age Range: 8 – 13
2 minutes   By Joyce Storey

You don't understand. I loooooove baseball. I know every stat on, like, every player ever! My dad and I've been going to watch the Yankees since I can remember. We have our own jerseys and caps and everything. And I take my glove in case I catch a pop fly. I came close once, but I wasn't tall enough and this big guy caught it. We always sit in the nosebleed section. My dad calls it that cuz it's so high in the stands. We race to see who can climb the stairs the fastest. I always win. It's way fun up there and when the guy comes around with hotdogs and soda, my dad always buys me some. I don't think there's a hotdog around that tastes better. So you see, Miss Williams, there's no way I can be here for a test tomorrow. It's the season opener! And my dad has tickets! How can you give me a zero if I'm not here? You sooooo don't get it! The season opener is, like, the best day of the year! I can't miss that! And my parents will be mad if I get a zero on my test. I'm totally afraid to tell my dad cuz he'll be sooooo disappointed if I miss out. And what if the Yankees win? What then? I'll be missing history! And that would be a tragedy. In 10 years I won't remember what was on the test, but I'll remember if the Yankees won. How about I write a book report about it when I come back? That would be as good as a test, right? I'll do a bibliography and

everything! I'll be really professional like a journalist or something. And if I catch the ball, I'll give it to you. What do you say? Deal?

*NOTE: You can substitute whatever baseball team you like. Pick your favorite and have fun!

SHOPPING

Female Dramatic
Age Range: 11 – 18
2 minutes   By Talia Pura

Why is it that every time I think I have an answer for
something, I don't? My mother told me that Aunt Cindy
was depressed and I should spend some time with her.
I thought that shopping would be the perfect thing to
cheer her up. We could try on clothes and she could
buy me something — just like when I was little. Turns
out that there are things that shopping can fix, and
things it can't. We used to have so much fun. She was
not fun this morning. Finally, we stopped for lunch. I
decide to take the direct approach and ask her what
is bothering her. She tells me that she thinks life is
passing her by. She always thought that she would get
married and have kids one day, just like my mom. But
now she feels like it's too late, like it will never happen
for her. I suggest that there is always foreign adoption.
It works for movie stars. She can save a baby from
some other poor country. She says it's too expensive.
Besides, she wants the perfect husband to go with the
perfect baby. I have nothing to say to that. I don't see
any perfect guy hanging around waiting to marry her. I
don't see any guys hanging around her at all. Not to be
mean about it, or anything. I hate this. Why do grown-
ups tell us their problems? I'm just a kid. I've got all the
time in the world, don't I? Am I going to be Aunt Cindy
one day? Having fun, doing everything I want to do and
then waking up one morning all depressed because it's
too late to have a baby and I'm tired of being alone?
(*pause*) Great, now I'm depressed, too.

SLEEPWALKING

Male/Female Comedic
Age Range: 6 – 12
1.5 minutes   By Talia Pura

Sometimes I walk in my sleep. It's the weirdest thing. How can a person get out of bed and do stuff, but not even know that you're doing it? Eventually, I wake up. I've found myself in the strangest places. Once, I woke up in the laundry room. I was trying to get into the clothes dryer. Another time, my mom woke me up because I was in the kitchen, banging on some pots and pans with a wooden spoon. It didn't even wake me up. Good thing I wasn't playing in the knife drawer. Sometimes, I don't wake up until the morning, and I find weird things in my bed, like my bike helmet, or my toothbrush, or once, I woke up wearing my snow boots. It's kind of freaky, isn't it? I mean, I go to bed and fall asleep, but can't seem to stay there. Apparently, I might grow out of it. Part of me hopes so, but part of me doesn't want to stop. It might be kind of boring to go through a whole night, night after night, without any adventures at all.

TALK TO ME

Female Comedic/Dramatic
Age Range: 8 – 12
1.5 minutes   By Talia Pura

Why is it so much easier to talk to someone with a message, instead of the phone, or even worse, in person? There's this cute boy in my class, and he looks at me all day, but whenever I look at him, he looks away like he doesn't want me to know he was looking at me. I LIKE him! I want him to look at me. I want him to TALK to me. Sometimes he mumbles "hey" when he "accidently" has to pass by me on his way to the pencil sharpener. Nobody in class has a dull pencil more often than him. But that's it. That's all he'll say until he gets homes from school and on his phone. Then we chat back and forth for hours. He tells me all kinds of things. We talk about homework, and his annoying brother, and who likes whom in our class, and he even tells me that he likes me. But, then I get to school in the morning, and he goes back to pretending he's not looking at me. This has been going on forever, like, at least a week! Tomorrow, I'm going to talk to him. I'm not going to wait for him to talk to me, 'cause that's never going to happen. I'm just going to march right up to him and say hello! No, I'm not. That's too scary. Maybe I'll just send him another message.

TEAM EFFORT

Male/Female Dramatic
Age Range: 9 – 16
2 minutes   By Talia Pura

Well, I think that went pretty well. I mean, I don't think I was actually brilliant, but I think I did okay. There were four more people than they need for the team. Those are pretty good odds. Aren't they? Only four of us will not make the team. What if they don't pick me? Maybe I did totally suck! How embarrassing to be one of only four who doesn't get picked. Only four! I really wish hundreds of kids had come to the try-outs. It would be way less embarrassing to be one of 200 not picked for the team. I actually don't care very much if I make it. You know who does care, right? My dad. He really cares. He always made the team for every sport, and he was always the star. He can hardly stand it that I'm not all that crazy about sports. Sometimes, I just really wish that I had a brother or sister, someone else to go out for team sports, instead of just me. What if I don't make it? How can I go home and tell my dad? This is the first year that I've even tried. I ran out of excuses not to… I think I could enjoy this sport if I gave it a chance. My dad practiced with me for the last two weeks. He's got a lot riding on this. I'm not sure if he'll recover if I don't make the team. That's the thing with parents, right? You've got to be so careful with them, because they can get their feelings hurt so easily. I guess I'll just start working on my "I didn't get picked" speech, just in case it doesn't work out. I hope he understands that there's always next year.

TEASED

Female Dramatic
Age Range: 10 – 14
2 minutes   By Talia Pura

I thought this year would be different. Some of the other girls developed over the summer. And some of them are stuffing their bras now. But they are all still just teasing me. (*pause*) What nobody understands is that I like to flirt just like everyone else. I'd never actually do anything with a boy. But I don't think I'm a tease. What am I supposed to do when guys flirt with me? I guess I just assumed that they wanted to hang out with me, whether we hook up or not. I didn't think I was leading them on; I just thought we were friends. Is that the only reason they hang out with me, so they can hook up with me? Sometimes, I'm curious what it's like to kiss a certain guy. If I do kiss him, I'm a you-know-what; if I don't, I'm a tease. I really just want to be treated like a normal person. So, I'm trying a whole "be nice no matter what" thing. No matter what mean thing someone says, I'll be nice back. I will be nice to everyone, all the time. I made a list of rules to live by: Be nice, or at least nonchalant, to everyone. Never make fun of losers. Sing in the shower — just 'cause it feels good. Let people vent on you. Make sure your deodorant works. Don't trust guys who are full of themselves. Don't talk about yourself too much. Keep a diary and read it when you get old — that's what I do already. I don't want a boyfriend right now; I just want friends. Some of the girls actually think I enjoy it when all the guys hassle me. They even think it's my fault that I'm teased. Maybe, if I follow these rules, I'll get all my old friends back.

TELL ME WHAT YOU REALLY THINK

Female Dramatic
Age Range: 9 – 12
2 minutes   By Talia Pura

My best friend hid behind the sofa at the sleepover last night. We weren't playing hide-and-seek or anything. I was having a sleepover for all my friends in my parents' RV, parked in the driveway. All of us, except for Megan Smith and my best friend Jody, went into the house to get some snacks. When we came back to the RV, Megan said that Jody went home because she had a stomachache. I thought that was weird. She'd been fine half an hour ago. But, whatever, I was about to call her, to see if she was okay, but Megan started asking all of us what we thought of Jody. She's my best friend and is usually very nice to me. We have a lot of fun together. She makes me laugh all the time. Some of the other girls said that she always thinks she knows everything, and some other stuff that wasn't very nice. I stuck up for her though, even though they are kind of right about her, too. And then, she popped her head up from behind the sofa and scared us all half to death. I couldn't believe she did that! She said that she just wanted everyone's honest opinion. Awkward. I'd never think of doing anything like that. No one knew what to say. I'll bet she wished she could go home with a stomachache then, but that would have been doubly weird, so she stayed. I think there are some things you are better off just not knowing.

THE HOARDER

Male/Female Comedic
Age Range: 7 – 11
2 minutes   By Joyce Storey

Mom, my room is really messy. Do you think I'm a hoarder? I just watched an episode about it on YouTube. Have you ever seen it, Mom? These people have lots and lots of stuff and keep it all in the house and some of them keep it in their garages, too. But I don't have a garage. I just have a room. And it's really, really messy. It's supposed to be a sickness, hoarding. Do you think I have that or do you think you don't get to be a hoarder until you have a whole house? I have lots of stuff but I really, really like it all. Do you think we should give it away to all the sick children in the world? But maybe the sick children wouldn't want it. Did you ever think of that? I mean, they're sick — so maybe they don't want to play with all my toys. And I really, really like my toys. Do you think I have to give them all away, so I won't be a hoarder anymore? I know you spent a lot of money on all that stuff and I really, really appreciate it. I really, really do, Mom. But I don't want to be a hoarder when I grow up and I don't want to be a kid hoarder either and what if I have kids and they become hoarders? These are important questions, Mom. What? Really? You think I just need to clean up my room and that will fix everything? Really? I mean really, really? Yesssss! So, I'm not a hoarder! That's really, really good news. I'm going to go start now. I can't wait to be a normal kid again! Oh, and about the sick kids — maybe I will give one toy to one sick kid. How about that? I got cured really, really fast and maybe they will, too.

TITLE PAGE

Male/Female Comedic
Age Range: 6 – 12
1 minute   By Talia Pura

Arrrg! I can't stand it. If I have to make one more project cover, I'm going to scream. I like doing my homework, but why does everything have to have a title page? I can't draw, all right? My teacher says everyone can draw, and mine look great. Right! She's paid to say that. It's not true. I did a project about cats, so my title page has to have a picture of a cat. I tried to hand it in with the word CATS across the middle of the page. The letters were really neat. I worked on them. She handed it back and said I needed to draw a picture, too. I downloaded one from the Internet and she said it didn't count. Arrrg! It's almost bedtime and I have to get this finished. Too bad my cat is going to look just like last week's rabbit and last month's snowman. Oh well, she asked for it, so that's what she's going to get.

TOBOGGANING

Male/Female Comedic
Age Range: 8 – 12
2 minutes   By Talia Pura

(*calling to someone off stage*) Yeah, okay, see you at four o'clock. (*turns away from friend*) Here we go again. Great. I just promised to go tobogganing at four o'clock. It's just about the last thing I want to do, but I have to. Who invented tobogganing anyway? Whose idea was it to make kids pile onto a toboggan and go hurtling down a hill? There is always some stupid bump on the hill, or a rock or something that the toboggan runs over and everyone goes flying off the toboggan. We all land in a heap in the snow. And no matter what, no matter where I sit on the toboggan, in the front, in the back or in the middle, I ALWAYS end up at the bottom of the heap. There is snow up my nose, the wind is knocked out of me, I feel like I've broken an arm or a leg, or both and the biggest kid on the toboggan lands on my head. Always. Every. Single. Time. But I can't just say I don't want to go tobogganing because then they'll think I'm weird. Everybody I know is just crazy about tobogganing and when we finally get enough snow, they can't wait to head to the hill and away we go. I'm doomed. All I can do now is hope for an early spring.

VIDEO GAME

Male/Female Comedic/Dramatic
Age Range: 7 – 12
1.5 minutes   By Joyce Storey

There's this video game I want. It's called *Ghost Recon Wildlands*. It's really cool. I wanted to be the first one in my class to get it, but Darius beat me to it. So now I gotta get it soon, so I can top his score. Besides, it's an awesome game. All the players are members of the "Ghosts." They're this special operations command. You know, kinda like the Delta Force. And you use all these awesome military weapons and kick butt! And it's got dirt bikes and helicopters and dune buggies, but the best part is the drones that tag your enemies and give you objectives. You upgrade them as you go and stuff. Cool, right? Come on, Mom, it's educational. I'm learning all about strategic thinking. Isn't that what you said you do at your job? And in the game you go through mountains and forests and deserts and salt flats. Yeah, salt flats. You know, flats with salt. It's like traveling the world in one video game. Think of all the money it would cost to take me around the world. And I'm just asking for one little game. It's economically a much better deal for you. So Jody gave me $20 for my birthday and I saved $10 from my allowance. Do you think you could kick in the rest? I heard Dad say he's getting his bonus soon. Whatta you say?

WHAT DO I WANT TO BE?

Male/Female Comedic
Age Range: 8 – 15
1 minute   By Talia Pura

What do I want to be when I grow up? Why? What could it possibly matter to you? Is that what you ask every kid you meet? I think I've heard that question 50 times just this week. I've started saying that I want to be a mortician, just to see the expression on their faces. They must think I never read. Maybe a kid isn't supposed to know what a mortician is. I was kind of surprised when I first read about one. And no, I don't think I want to put makeup on dead people when I grow up. I think that's the creepiest thing I've ever heard of. But, is it worth saying I want to be a mortician just to watch the big cheesy grin wiped off an adult's face? Absolutely. Go ahead. Make my day. Ask me what I want to be when I grow up.

MEET THE AUTHORS

JOYCE STOREY

Joyce Storey is an award-winning writer, producer, and actor. Her plays *Caged* and *Time Wars* have been produced in New York City. Other plays include: *The Best That Mother Knows* and *Dirty Laundry*. Screenplays include: *Guardian Angel, Blind Allie, Run Away Forever, Enchanted Forrest* and *Thirty G's*. Her films have won awards both nationally and internationally. She has written for such publications as: *The Guardian, Front of House Magazine, Live Sound International*, and *PLSN Magazine*. Her column, *Joyce Of The Theatre*, has been read by more than 40,000 subscribers. She has written travel videos and audio tours for the *Your Guide Around* series, including: *Your Guide Around NYC, The Empire State Building, Times Square,* and *Prince Edward Island*. Her work has been published internationally in such anthologies as: *Holding Onto Forever* and *Pearls Of The Past*. Her poetry has been chosen for publication in the International Library of Poetry's *The Best Poems and Poets*. She has several projects in development, including a new musical as well as her first novel. She holds a bachelor's degree from Acadia University, a Producer's Certificate from Dov Simens Film School and a Filmmaker's Certificate from the Digital Film Academy in New York. Joyce is the founder of MonologuesToGo.com and is a proud member of the Dramatists Guild and SAG-AFTRA. She is a recipient of the Terry Fox Humanitarian Award and is cited in the Marquis *Who's Who of American Women*. Joyce resides in New York City with her Tony Award-winning husband, Howell Binkley.

TALIA PURA

Talia Pura is a playwright, actor, director, filmmaker, designer, aerial dancer and educator. She has written/produced/directed 10 short dramatic films, which have been screened at various film festivals around the world, with some licensed for television broadcasts on the Canadian Broadcasting Corporation (CBC). As a playwright, Talia has written more than 25 plays, resulting in many productions, several publications, and a CBC radio commission. *Cry After Midnight*, based on her experiences as a Canadian Forces war artist in Afghanistan, represented Canada at the Women Playwrights International Conference (WPIC) in Stockholm in 2012 and was read at the Canadian War Museum in Ottawa in 2013. She performed her solo drama, *This I Have Believed,* at the WPIC in Cape Town in 2015. She has also staged many of her other solo dramas, including *Confessions of an Art School Model*, which she toured extensively, including a run at the New York Fringe Festival. Her book, *STAGES: Creative Ideas For Teaching Drama* was published by J. Gordon Shillingford Publishing, Inc. in 2002, with a revised edition published in 2013, along with *CUES: Theatre Training and Projects from Classroom to Stage*. Her children's book, *Alexia Wants to Fly*, was published in 2015. Talia has appeared in many feature films, television shows and independent shorts. A highlight is her work with Guy Maddin in *The Saddest Music in the World* and *Sombra Dolorosa*. As a theatrical costume and set designer, she is partial to period pieces. Her aerial dance on silks includes solos with everything from symphony orchestras to rock bands, and a film commission from the 2010 Vancouver Olympic Games. After teaching high school drama for many years, she spent 15 years teaching theater at the Department of Education at the University of Winnipeg. She has enjoyed leading workshops in her own brand of devised theater in Canada, the U.S., Thailand, the Philippines, South Africa, and Brazil. Talia holds a Masters of Arts in creative writing from the University of Manitoba. A proud member of The Dramatists Guild and SAG-AFTRA, she lives in Santa Fe, New Mexico, with her visual artist/composer husband, William Pura. (www.taliapura.com)

NOTES

Made in the USA
Columbia, SC
16 October 2020